GREATNESS IS
WHAT
GREATNESS DOES

GREATNESS IS **WHAT** GREATNESS DOES

The 10 Principles of Exceptional Leadership in the Quantum Psychology Perspective

RONALD T. HICKEY
DR. OLLIE R. MACK

HICKEY HOUSE BOOKS

Published by Hickey House Books

GREATNESS IS WHAT GREATNESS DOES
The 10 Principles of Exceptional Leadership
in the Quantum Psychology Perspective
Copyright © 2024 by Ronald T. Hickey

All rights reserved. This book may not be reproduced in whole or in part without written permission from the publisher, except by a reviewer who may quote brief passages in an article or a review; nor may any part of this book be reproduced, stored in a retrieval system, or transmitted in any form or by any means, electronic, mechanical, photocopying, recording, or other, without written permission from the publisher.

For information address: Hickey House Books,
1079 Sunrise Ave, Ste. B-205, Roseville, CA 95661.
Trademarks appearing in the book are the property of their respective owners and are used only to identify them and/or their products and services.

Greatness Is What Greatness Does™ is a trademark owned by Ronald T. Hickey
Printed in the United States of America.
10 9 8 7 6 5 4 3 2 1
ISBN 978-0-9856139-6-9
Editor: Scribendi
Hickey House Books
Roseville, California 95661
www.hickeyhousebooks.com

Library of Congress Cataloging-in-Publication Data
Hickey, Ronald T. (Ronald Terrence), 1964-
Greatness is what greatness does: the 10 principles
of exceptional leadership, in the quantum psychology
perspective/Ronald T. Hickey.
—1st ed.
p.cm.
ISBN 978-0-9856139-6-9 2024919279

To my Redeemer for continuing to love me for who I am. You have encouraged me to come higher. Thank You for Your grace and mercy!

To my children for inspiring me to be greater every day. My own greatness has always flowed directly from your brilliance. I learned everything I know about leadership from seeing and watching each of you grow.

To everyone I have ever led, without which this book would not have been possible. Your faith, belief, and courage to boldly follow me and offer your insightful critiques are truly what has made this work possible. The readers, along with me, are intrinsically indebted.

Table of Contents

Introduction
Greatness Is What Greatness Does   1

Principle 1
Perception: Who you are matters   13

Principle 2
Relationships: Exceptional relationships are the bedrocks of exceptional leadership   30

Principle 3
Inspiration: An exceptional leader inspires a shared vision   51

Principle 4
NOW: A great leader must be in the NOW   68

Principle 5
Complete: The exceptional leader is complete   89

Principle 6
Intensity: Exceptional leadership is exceptionally intense   107

Principle 7
People, Processes, and Paradigms   122

Principle 8
Leadership: The exceptional leader leads the way   150

Principle 9
Expectations: The exceptional leader has high expectations   172

Principle 10
Strategy: The exceptional leader must have a strategic plan   190

INTRODUCTION

Greatness Is What Greatness Does

What is greatness in human interaction? What is greatness in leadership, and what does greatness in leadership look like in action? The concept of greatness is an amalgamation of wisdom, experimentation, experience, and tacit knowledge that offers great insights into these questions, and others, for every individual who may be contemplating greatness in leadership. The author and contributor of this literary work have traversed the landscape of our nation, the land of opportunity, coast to coast and north to south times over; we are authors, a publisher, motivators, human capacity engineers, leadership development consultants, Ph.D. holders, HR professionals, senior executives, organizational performance management consultants, a psychologist, retired assistant superintendent of public schools, business owners, intellectuals, scholars, and many other things. We have presented and executed our skills in various professional and social settings, and the diversity of Americans who have honored us with their attendance includes every race, culture, national heritage, socioeconomic condition, personal and professional success, religion, mental disposition, and anthropoid desire available in the American demography. We have also traveled extensively on six of the world's seven continents. Our life interactions, as with many Americans, extend vertically and horizontally in a universal fashion. As great Americans, we have served our great nation as members of the United States Armed Forces and as politicians. We have worked as engineers, electricians, law enforcement officers, educators, medical professionals, CEOs, attorneys, and local community leaders. We have also mopped floors, served food, managed others, and sat in board rooms. Dr. Ollie R. Mack and I, collectively, have had and are having career paths that encompass all the human attributes listed above. In our combined lives, we have led in every possible way a human can lead and be led. Ollie, and I, both African American men, emerged from the southern regions of the United States from very meager beginnings to now stand at the very pinnacle of financial success and professional achievement. Greatness is not necessarily defined by the finish line but, in most cases, the starting line. The two of us who passionately offer this work of literature on leadership greatness have lives that began in some of the most horrid human conditions. While the starting line was less than desirable, we were pushed into greatness as a result. "What is greatness?" you may ask. *Greatness Is What Greatness Does*. This is the title of this great book on leadership. Everyone can become a great leader. Great leaders are not born great leaders. They are made by their circumstances and dogged will to be great in life and leadership.

We are not destined at birth in the United States of America. In America, a man or woman can self-impose fervent personal desire upon their individual life and recast and reshape the cosmographic projections of what they will become, essentially being in total control of the quality and quantity of one's life. My vast and privileged leadership experiences and the collective leadership experiences of contributor Dr. Ollie R. Mack have extended to this work on leadership an intimate human knowledge and provided thought leadership and extensive observations of an enormous array of human conditions. In our other-people-centered contemplations of every human situation we have encountered, we have concluded that Americans at the extremes and in the masses have viable access to tremendous opportunities for living handsome lives and are simultaneously in a constant state of wanting more than the abundance they already possess. How does one successfully lead an organization in such an American culture rot with entitlement and privilege? How does one evolve into a great leader in the American culture of mediocrity and minimum standards? Leadership can be a very strange and peculiar dichotomy in social environments in which individuals under your brand of leadership already have more than others around the globe and are simultaneously unequivocally unsatisfied. The wealth of many Americans is absolutely obscene. This abominable condition of financial means of many Americans stands in stark contrast to the crippling levels of poor self-worth conveyed by so many other Americans. How does one successfully lead their corporation in such conditions of income inequality? We are a nation of individuals prone to endless folly and insatiable desire. We tend to be equally satisfied and dissatisfied to the extent of our perceived comparisons to others. Our dissatisfactions are not isolated to global desires to be the best in the world. Our innate insatiable dynamics extend into our everyday lives as well. It is not enough to be living in the best country; as Americans, we need to live in the best suburban areas and have the biggest houses in the neighborhood. We must have the largest accumulation of financial wealth in our immediate circle. Our automobiles must be better, however better is defined, than the neighbors' vehicles. Our kids must go to a better school than the children of our friends and acquaintances. If someone we know has a swimming pool in their backyard, then we must construct a bigger swimming pool, even if bigger equates to only a few inches. By being so overwhelmingly influenced by the expand and contract, live-for-today, hotel culture of infinite want impregnated by the "New Jack City" American dream, we have suppressed the narrative of our lives and dangerously impoverished the human spirit and our individual souls, insomuch as the connection to the humanity of others is very strained. In the process, we have severely challenged our ability to reframe the context of our future; for in America, more is better, bigger is the goal, winning is the only option, and uncontrollable desire is king. This is the American way of life! Dr. Ollie Mack and I have one simple question: "What does greatness in leadership in a country overwhelmed by such personal self-interest look like in action?" *Greatness Is What Greatness Does.*

This really is a book on leadership, but we must first develop a full description of the conditions one must consider when stepping into a leadership role. So, who we are matters. Who the leader is matters. Who is being led matters. Every great leader possesses an insatiable and incessant desire to be highly successful in life and at work. Every great leader is also a handsomely talented individual who strives to maximize the performance of others. The professional and social environments in which most leaders operate provide profound challenges to their desires to succeed and rise to their maximum levels of performance. Why does leading others to maximum levels of performance, more often than not, seem so daunting of a task? The human conditions in which one leads determine the road ahead. Quantum psychology would suggest that people are so intrinsically unique at the tiniest molecular level that our

INTRODUCTION: GREATNESS IS WHAT GREATNESS DOES

individual perceptions, desires, opinions, and principles make a group of people coming together and agreeing completely upon common goals and shared interests humanly impossible. In essence, simply being human and having to deal with other humans present an overwhelming challenge to great leadership. Insightful and placid identification of characteristics of the individual human suggests that our species is guaranteed to fail in all group dynamics if left without a set of guiding principles that lead us down the path to greatness, especially when faced with the entitlement and privileged culture. The question becomes, "Just how many exceptional principles does it take to guarantee the group will succeed?" Is it 1, 2, 3, 4, 5, 6, or even more? If you are great at something, and you are guided by the right set of principles, you should produce something great. Greatness really is what greatness does. Greatness does not fail; greatness succeeds to the maximum level. Therefore, greatness is maximum success, and greatness must be exceptionally principled.

The exceptional principles of exceptional leaders identify them as such and provide insight as to the quality of their leadership. America, because of our diversity in thought, expectations, perceptions, culture, class, education, desires, and wants, is an extremely challenging country to be an organization's leader. In such diversity, there is no commonly accepted definition of success. Success has taken on a plethora of looks in America, depending on who the judge may be and the instrument used to measure success. Nevertheless, highly successful people act habitually in exceptional manners and with exceptional principles that identify them as highly successful humans. If you were to study the daily activities of any person, you would eventually be able to isolate principles in their life that determine and construct the efficacy in the quality and quantity of their existence. There are particular rules and values in the life of a man who is a terrific husband and outstanding father that separates him from men who are not good husbands or good fathers. We know what a great woman and great mother looks like. Our adopted principles make us who we are. The exceptional rules and values followed by a great CEO of a great Fortune 500 company will be majorly different from the rules and values followed by a mediocre leader of a mediocre company. There are always particular and very distinctive principles for success in the life of a person who has achieved greatness in their life that differentiates them from the masses. *Greatness Is What Greatness Does.* There are particular and very distinctive principles that are followed in the life of a woman who has bent the arc of history to become the first female vice president of the United States. There are particular and very distinctive patterns, rules, and values adopted in the life of a man who has admirably overcome insurmountable odds to become the first African American president of the United States of America. Great people do great things because they are guided by great principles. Great leaders are exceptional because they possess exceptional principles with which they guide their own lives and, eventually, the lives of those they lead.

Greatness Is What Greatness Does: The 10 Principles of Exceptional Leadership is a literary work that engages the rules and truths that produce exceptional leaders in a framework of 10 exceptional principles. The 10 principles establish a process for the leadership development of great leaders and great performance of others in this American culture of abundance and uncontrollable want. The principles provide for the development of new human behaviors, thus the creation of new

INTRODUCTION: GREATNESS IS WHAT GREATNESS DOES

life principles to lead with and live by within an American workforce conditioned with humans of extreme talents, begging for great leadership. While all humans desire success to a great degree and develop habits to a large degree, we must understand that what works for one does not necessarily work for others and, not all habits lead to the levels of success one seeks. It's easy for one to say, "Here are the habits of a highly successful person. Go repeat these habits, and you too will be highly successful." But it's not easy to change your ways and deploy such habits of highly successful people and make them work in your life, despite your determination and drive. If the endeavor was as easy of a task as it sounds, everyone would be highly successful in life. Well, there are definite reasons a person cannot simply take on the habits of others and experience the level of success that those others have experienced with the same habits. We are all different, and leaders in America must recognize that what worked 20 or 30 years ago is not going to work today. The people being led are different, and the leaders are different. We are muscling our way through severe health pandemics, social unrest extremes, political warfare, and climate change. How do we behave as great leaders in such challenging times? *Greatness Is What Greatness Does* explains in great details why success is far more than an exercise in simply reading about and attempting to repeat the patterns of others. Imagine being a great leader just for a moment. While holding the image of your greatness vividly in your mind, realize that there is only one you, and there can be no one else like you. This also means that you cannot be anyone else, despite your wildest aspirations. You have your own unique references, opinions, principles, and perceptions when you embark upon any attempt of self-development and self-evaluation. Now consider what principles could guide you to your greatness in leadership.

The 10 principles of exceptional leadership that will be expanded upon in this book are as follows:

Principle 1 – **Perception: Who you are matters.**

Principle 2 – **Relationships: Exceptional relationships are the bedrocks of exceptional leadership.**

Principle 3 – **Inspiration: An exceptional leader inspires a shared vision.**

Principle 4 – **NOW: A great leader must be in the NOW—navigating with organizational focus and a worldview.**

Principle 5 – **Complete: The exceptional leader is complete. He or she is cubic—of equal measure in the length, width, and height of their leadership.**

Principle 6 – **Intensity: Exceptional leadership is exceptionally intense. Intensity pushes you to your maximum. It pushes you to be exceptional in everything you do.**

Principle 7 – **People, Processes, and Paradigms: The exceptional leader creates performance paradigms with exceptional people and processes in mind.**

Principle 8 – **Leadership: The exceptional leader leads the way by modeling exceptional leadership behaviors and skills.**

Principle 9 – **Expectations: The exceptional leader has high expectations.**

Principle 10 – **Strategy: The exceptional leader must have a strategic plan that guides and informs organizational behaviors. A properly designed strategy leads the organization along a value continuum that leads to a specific vision of success.**

INTRODUCTION: GREATNESS IS WHAT GREATNESS DOES

The 10 principles of exceptional leadership recognize your uniqueness and reconstitute you into the absolute best version of yourself. As leaders, especially exceptional leaders, we are unable to clone our leadership after the leadership of others. There will never be another Steve Jobs. There will never be another Bill Gates. There will never be another President Barrack Obama. There will never be another you. You must succeed as you. Your greatness must do what it is capable of doing. In your unique leadership, you have established particular rules that you follow as a leader. That's why you are the leader you are. These rules that you follow have provided you with whatever you have and constructed you into whoever you are. Your level of education, the development of your natural talents and abilities, and your status in life all result from these patterns, principles, and rules. To create a better and improved you, you must establish a new set of patterns in your life. To create an exceptional leader in yourself, you must engage and develop a new set of exceptional principles to guide your life and leadership. Still, with the image of yourself as a great leader vividly held in your imagination, consider the quality and complexity of the undertaking when you attempt to suppress your mature habits in life while simultaneously attempting to create new ones by learning new principles. You must perform a circus act of sorts. In these acts, you juggle competing sets of principles. During these circus routines, you must morph into a leader who is led by a variety of principles. Your life goes from being guided by a few principles to being guided by many principles as a leader. You must change how you normally walk and talk, balance your mind, and consider your perceptions to ensure you develop the principles that will lead you down the path toward your greatness. This principled act demonstrates a major shift from your normal human habits. Change does not come easily. Eliminating familiar habits while simultaneously implementing new habits is very challenging indeed. Leading other people can exasperate your senses. As Jocko Willink stated, *"Leading people is the most challenging and, therefore, the most gratifying undertaking of all human endeavors."* To implement a sundry of new habits and principles simultaneously presents even greater leadership challenges. *Greatness Is What Greatness Does* challenges you to do just that.

Greatness Is What Greatness Does challenges you to embrace and develop 10 new exceptional leadership principles. You cannot leave any one of these principles undeveloped or under-developed without potential imperil to your leadership greatness. Developing the 10 principles of exceptional leadership requires fervent determination and clear vision. We know from quantum psychology that who we are is both a reference and a challenge to the leader we desire to become. Our mature human habits tend to exist as the self-imposed limitations to our leadership greatness and our maximum personal and professional development. To transition into greatness, one must first identify and deal with oneself. Until one does so, recreating an all-new great leader is practically futile. Limitations have this uncanny ability to hold us at bay from where we want to be. Remember, it is perhaps the starting line that matters most in life. The reason for our mental self-stultification is that we simply refuse to challenge ourselves to understand our personal limits, truths, and perceptions and how our beliefs affect others that we lead. We do not easily adopt new principles. Often times, as humans, our limits are simply our own thoughts in reference to ourselves. We don't believe we can overcome the obstacles that stare us in the face. We're not sure if we are as

INTRODUCTION: GREATNESS IS WHAT GREATNESS DOES

brilliant as we say we are. We don't know if we have enough talent. In essence, we don't understand ourselves at the molecular level. Until you can define unequivocally what makes you the leader that you are, you cannot viably consider transitioning your leadership to a level of greatness. Understanding your perceptions and acknowledging and respecting others' perceptions is the foundation of great leadership. That is the first principle of exceptional leadership—who we are matters.

As mentioned in the beginning of this introduction, the writers of this book have an enormous range of experience in human capacity engineering. Our paths to greatness have been as unique to our journey to greatness as we are unique in who we are. Greatness is a destination; get there! It is a mindset; create it! It is a lifestyle; live it! This book, *Greatness Is What Greatness Does*, was developed on this very principle: *The quality and quantity of one's leadership is subjugated by one's willingness to develop a leadership style committed to a variety of exceptional principles. How well one maintains an equal balance of these powerful and transformative principles will ultimately determine if, and to what degree, they succeed in leadership.* This is not a book designed to be a one-size-fits-all type of read. As stated earlier, your reward will equal your effort. Are you up for the challenge? The 10 principles of exceptional leadership will provide you the necessary quantum psychological insights into your own psyche and an understanding of just how powerful your God-given talents, personal ambitions, and passionate visions truly are. You will embrace the fact that you have the mental toughness to accept challenges and emerge a better, more improved leader. You will learn that properly aligning your leadership talents, ambitions, and passions with sound principles will deliver you to any level of greatness that you dare to set your sights on.

This book will assist you in self-liberating the anecdote of your leadership, which is one of the very reasons we walk this earth. If you embrace the principles and accept the challenges, and I know you will, you will move far beyond your self-imposed leadership limits, and you shall be liberated from everything preventing your greatness. You will emerge with new principles that will forever connect you to the idea that you are as brilliant, gorgeous, talented, and fabulous as anyone who has ever lived and led. Your leadership is your autobiography. Your leadership path is your wisdom; walk it. Your leadership success is your beauty; groom it. The leader you become will be determined by who you are right now and by the new principles you develop, starting today; for *Greatness Is What Greatness Does.*

PRINCIPLE ONE

Perception

Perception: Who You Are Matters

"It's not what you are looking at that matters; it's what you see."

—Henry David Thoreau

Perception is the view of reality. Reality becomes the truth. Truth is what you see, given the unique lens through which circumstances are viewed, and everyone has a unique set of lenses with which life is viewed. A thousand individuals can observe the same object, and all one thousand see it differently. Sight is subjugated by focus. One sees what one intends to see. In leadership, as in life, who you are matters; for who you are determines how you view your world. Who you are determines what you focus on. Who you are determines how you engage others around you. Who you are determines what you see and how you engage it. Who you are even determines what you see as you drive your vehicle on a busy roadway. The next time you are driving down the highway, consider how many vehicles are on the highway with you, moving in both directions; some passing by you, and others you are passing. Then think for a moment about how many of the moving vehicles you can accurately describe. Of the hundreds of cars on the roadway with you, you can only accurately describe the ones you focused on;

the ones you intentionally observe. You see them all in your peripheral vision, but you really see only the ones you aim to see. And what you aim to see is predicated on who you are. Who you are matters. Quantum psychology states that "You cannot remove the individual from the description of the observation." In leadership, you cannot remove the leader from the description of the observation because who the leader is, his and her perceptions, matters the most in describing their leadership. In the vehicle, driving down the freeway as described above, the driver and the passengers have individual separate experiences, even though they are traveling in the same car. Our individual perception ensures that our capabilities as humans are a congener to our unique set of truths, values, and rules—our principles—and how we see our surroundings. Once you realize that your perceptions determine who you are and what you see, you will instinctively understand the potential greatness in your leadership abilities.

Putting in the work and discovering and understanding who you are, what you see, what your principles are, and your perceptions at the molecular level are absolutely necessary if you desire to reach your full unbridled leadership potential. The knowledge of self, knowing who you are at the most miniscule of your psychological qualities, establishes the reference point from which your leadership grows. If you do not understand what drives your life and what drives those you lead, then you cannot quantify your ability to lead your team. Here is a practical illustration: If you log on to the internet and go to the Yahoo or Google website to access a map search engine, the first bit of information the map search engine asks for is your starting point. If you do not know your starting point, the search engine will not allow you to simply enter a destination and obtain accurate directions. You must enter a starting address and a destination address. At that point, the map will provide you with clear directions for your travels as long as both points are recognizable addresses. Your leadership growth and professional endeavors operate in an identical manner. You cannot simply say you want to become a great leader or a phenomenal CEO of your company and then ask the universe for a successful process for greatness. You cannot simply say you want to become an impassioned senior executive in isolation of your core personal principles, values, and truths. You cannot become a great motivator of subordinate personnel or an inspirational leader of the 72 million millennials who now dominate the workforce, void of the perceptions of others, and expect the universe to provide you with the road map to greatness. You must first understand whether you have the psychological qualities at the molecular level and the innate talents and abilities to work with the perceptions of other humans to become a great leader, a phenomenal CEO, an impassioned motivator, or an inspirational leader.

Who you are and what you see, your perceptions, matter the most in determining the directions you must travel and the processes you must follow to become the great leader you strongly desire to become. Who you are determines if the journey is possible. Being an exceptional author with the ability to write this book has associated educational prerequisites. Do you have the required imagination and subject matter expertise to become a world-renowned author and motivational speaker? Becoming an astronaut requires you to possess certain physical and mental abilities. Do you possess such abilities? Neal Armstrong was not the average everyday person. He, like all astronauts, possessed some specific talents, ambitions, and visions for becoming such. An artist must have a creative imagination. Do you have such an imagination? Becoming a company's CEO requires a plethora of professional attributes. Do you meet those requirements? In all circumstances, knowing who and where you are determines the direction you must travel to become who you desire to be or get to where you desire to go. However, just like the internet search engines, you must enter the information that establishes where you are in your leadership before you can obtain accurate directions for where you want to go. After all, you cannot remove the leader from the description of the leadership, and the leader must be able to see what she intends to see.

A Perspective on Leadership: *My mother taught me to always have a sound understanding of who I am. She always said, "Life has a way of forcing you down paths you never intended to travel. Understanding who you are will allow you to get back on track when you find yourself traveling in the wrong direction." Knowing who I am means I am never lost in the workplace. It is a constant reminder that my individual perceptions may not be anyone else's reality. My reality may not be another's truth. My truth may not be how another person views the world. As a senior executive in my company, it is important that I never lose sight of my perspective and that of others. Human resources are the people competency of the organization. I must see every employee as an individual with individual sets of values, needs, interests, and opinions. I must never be lost as a leader because my misdirections can be a detriment to the organization's morality. In reference to my superiors and subordinates, I always know who I am and how my perceptions impact my decisions and, ultimately, my organization. In your place of employment, in a team environment, knowledge of self-awareness is crucial. Far too many leaders lead in isolation; they very seldom consider the values,*

PRINCIPLE ONE: PERCEPTION

needs, interests, and opinions of others. Like on the freeway, they see others in their peripheral visions, but they do not see with intention, focus, and aim. An unexceptional leader will send out an email to 100 employees and expect everyone to perceive the email exactly as he or she intended for it to be perceived. Exceptional leaders must know who they are and know their 100 subordinates as well. They must have leadership sight that is subjugated by the proper aim.

Exercise: *At your next staff meeting, bring a lemon. Pass the lemon around and ask everyone to write down their individual descriptions of the lemon. Everyone must write down 10 points of description of the lemon. Direct the staff to touch, squeeze, smell, and look at the lemon. Once everyone has described their lemon, direct everyone to get up from their seats and find another person that described the lemon exactly word for word as they did. What you will discover is that no two people will describe a lemon in the exact same 10 terms of description. What you will discover is that there are no two staff members who possess the same set of values, needs, interests, opinions, or perceptions of a lemon. No two employees will see the lemon exactly the same. Therefore, all 100 employees from the perspective above can't possibly perceive the same message from the same email. Who we are matters the most in the workplace.*

Understand your talents, ambitions, and passions, as well as those of the people you are tasked to lead. Greatness in leadership is the degree to which you understand yourself in the "wilderness of your leadership." Constantly assess whether your perceptions complement the needs of the organization. Don't be afraid to answer honestly when the answer is "I don't know." If the answer is "I don't know," travel back to who you are. Get back to the basics of your sight and aim. Do not work in a position where you cannot fully satisfy the needs of the team, and the team cannot fully follow your lead. Play to your strengths. When Michael Jordan left the NBA for a career in Major League Baseball, he had the passion and ambition for the game, but he did not have the necessary talent to play baseball at the same Hall of Fame level he played in the NBA. He elected to give up his try at baseball because he understood that baseball could not satisfy his need to succeed at the same level at which he succeeded in the NBA. He understood that his talent level did not satisfy the needs of his team. Michael returned to the NBA. He knew who he was. He had sight subjugated by his aim. He had a sense of direction in his life because he understood who and where he was and understood who and where he wanted to be as an athlete. We all need to become more efficient at making similar assessments in our leadership. Far too many of us are not talented enough or ambitious enough or passionate enough in our leadership roles to become great leaders. As a result, our teams are suffering because we fail to meet their needs. Work should never be only about the paycheck if you expect any degree of greatness or high levels of leadership performance. Leadership greatness is the result of knowing who you are and who others around you are. You must be able to see greatness before you can become greatness.

> *"A leader is one who sees the way before others do, illuminates the way so others can see it, and leads the way so others can follow."*
>
> —Ronald T. Hickey

Your leadership should involve you constantly striving to better yourself, and success should bring about change in how you think and what you believe. Who you are should only be a reference point in your leadership, never the mark of your final destination of greatness. *Greatness Is What Greatness Does.*

PRINCIPLE ONE: PERCEPTION

Your leadership should be like a company's map, and your goal should be to travel every square inch of the company—*seeing the way, paving the way, and guiding the way*. It is extremely important for great leaders to touch every inch of the company, for one can only accurately describe what one is completely familiar with. In psychology, the observations of blind Sufis are used to demonstrate the importance of touching every inch of the company. In the infamous depiction, seven blind Sufis are positioned at different and separate locations around an elephant. One is positioned touching its tusk, one touching its trunk, one touching its back, one touching its stomach, one is touching its tail, one is touching an ear, and one touching a foot. Then each of the seven blind Sufis are asked to describe what they are touching. Each one can only describe the part of the elephant he is touching. And just like with the lemon exercise above, the seven blind Sufis can only describe what they are touching from their individual perception of what part of the elephant they are touching. Neither description is an accurate description of an elephant but only descriptions of the separate parts of the elephant. The only way one can accurately describe an elephant is to engage every inch of the elephant. The only process by which a leader can accurately describe her company is by touching every inch of the company. Only then can the leader see the way, pave the way, and guide the way accurately.

A Leadership Development Perspective: *In athletic sports competitions, as in leadership, you must see the play develop first. Once you see it, you must believe in what you see, and you must commit 100% to making the right decision. This type of insight is more about intuition and less about eyesight. You know yourself better* *than anyone else does. You know your abilities. You know your passion. You know your energy level. You know what you see. You must trust what you believe you know. When it comes to being or becoming great, you must trust that you have the abilities, passion, energy, and intuition to be or become great. Greatness really is what greatness does. A leader in an organization is like an NFL middle linebacker. As a middle linebacker in the NFL, a player must be patient in the defensive formation, stay in his lane, and wait until he sees the offensive play develop and lanes open up. Once he sees the gap in the offensive formation, he must believe in what he sees and, within seconds, shoot through the gap before it closes. Leadership greatness works in a similar fashion. A leader must practice patience, watch how operations develop, see the gap in business operations or organizational goals based on his or her perception and intuition, and shoot through the gap and make the right decision before the opportunity disappears. Leaders who can remain patient, develop great intuition, see the gap, and shoot through every time are going to do what greatness does. Great leaders believe in their intuition and shoot through the gap, just like an NFL middle linebacker.*

In my first book, *The Hoola Hoop Paradigm*, I wrote: "Years ago, I was hired as a portfolio manager at a collections agency. On the first day of employment, the owner of the company entered the orientation class and spoke to the group of us that had just been hired. He made a comment during his monologue that has made an impactful difference in my life ever since. Mr. Phillips described how he had failed at many things in his life until he discovered that he had a talent and passion for the collections business. He was very ambitious about his newly discovered talent and passion, and he decided to start his own collections agency. Ten years later, and millions of dollars in revenue later, Mr. Phillips was standing before the group of us addressing his newly hired employees. He challenged each and every one of us. He said, 'Ask yourself if you have an innate passion and natural talent for the collections business.' Mr. Phillips said, if you do not have passion and talent, you will never develop the necessary sight to become an ambitious collections agency employee." He said that success in the business would be mediocre at best without talent, passion, ambition, and foresight. Mr. Phillips went further and stated that the collections business is not the business to work in just to make a paycheck. I thought seriously about what my new boss had just said. I embraced the challenge he had just laid out before me. At the first break of the orientation class, I went to the personnel department and informed the personnel director that I no longer had any interest in employment with the company, and I left the building immediately. I was a portfolio manager at a collections agency for only two hours. That was my shortest tenure in employment at any company. I knew this type of employment was not the situation in which my talents and passions would be fully deployed. I could not see the gap. I did not see myself as a collection agent. Since that brief job, I have never again applied for or accepted a job that did not complement who I was, my talents, ambitions, passions, and foresight. As a result, I have been highly successful at all my places of employment. If you find that you are not or have not been successful in your leadership role, perhaps you need to discover just who you are and assess whether your employment choice compliments your talents, ambitions, passions, and vision. You may be engaged in an endeavor that has no potential for success and happiness for you. Discover who you are and understand what you see. Moreover, ask those you work with to do the same. Sit down with a pen and notebook or at your computer and complete the following challenge:

<u>The Perception Challenge:</u>
Describe yourself in 60 seconds.
List your leadership ambitions (every single one).
Write down your current vision for your life.
Write down your vision for your life 10 years from now.
If you had three wishes, list what you would wish for and why.
If today was your last day on earth, describe the entire last 24 hours of your life.
What has been your greatest joy in life?
Write down what has been your greatest regret in life.
List everything you cannot live without.
Write down everything you are afraid of.
Write the story of the worst time of your life.
What three things do you like the most about yourself?
Write a letter to your unborn great grandchildren to tell them what no one else will be able to tell them about you.
Now that you are beginning to develop an idea of who you are, do the following the very next day after you have completed the tasks above:
List five changes you would make in your life if you could today.
Of the five changes you list, commit to making one of those changes today. Then, commit to making the remaining changes within a year. Remember, greatness is an action. *Greatness Is What Greatness Does.*

I know this is a difficult and challenging list of questions to answer. Self-discovery can be a challenging and complex endeavor. Many of the items you have answered in the above exercises may represent questions you have never asked yourself. Some of the answers are downright painful to contemplate. Malcolm X once said, "*The examined life is painful.*" Avoiding the pain is why so many leaders are walking around not knowing who they truly are. This lack of self-knowledge is why many leaders are in unsatisfying situations at their places of employment and in their leadership roles. Our perceptions, talents, and abilities are misaligned, and we have blocked ourselves from finding our passion and pathways for great success. We have settled in jobs simply because the job pays the bills. We are in leadership positions that badly need to end because we don't have the esteem to do the work to get back to the path that leads to greatness, and mediocrity is not getting the job done. Many of us are leading teams that are marred in destitute situations because no one has a reference for the direction the team needs to travel. If you approach the above exercises in a serious manner, and if you are willing to be honest with yourself, you will find yourself in the "*wilderness of your leadership.*" In that wilderness is exactly where you will discover your leadership greatness. Take the information you provided in the exercise above and review and edit every one of them every single day for one month. I assure you; you will discover your leadership path to greatness and maximum leadership performance.

By no stretch of the imagination are the questions above suggested as the only questions or process to self-discovery. My hope is that this simply starts a dialogue with yourself that will last a lifetime. My hope is that you avoid wandering in the "wilderness of your leadership." This is similar to what Moses experienced as a leader when he freed the Israelites. After Moses freed the Israelites from bondage, the Christian Bible informs us that they wandered in the wilderness for 40 years.

When they finally made it to the promised land that Moses had spoken so fervently of for 40 years, they realized that every day for those 40 years, they had been only an 8-day travel away from their destination. The freed Israelites, once free, began to distrust Moses and others, despite trusting Moses enough to be led out of bondage. The Israelites forgot who they were as a people. They did not know who they were as individuals. Moses' leadership road map became unclear. They lost their way. So, for 40 years, they remained 8 days from their destination. In your leadership, do you trust the road map to great success, maximum performance, and the promise of greatness? Can you see where you are going? Is the destination your aim? Are you traveling your path to leadership greatness? Have you been wandering metaphorically for 40 years in your leadership when the destination is only 8 days away? The principle of perception and self-discovery will put you back on the right path. Self-discovery is the first step to your greatness because it establishes your foundation and starting point and will allow you to trust in your leadership abilities and in others' willingness to follow you. And a commitment to a lifetime of personal dialogue with yourself will ensure that the correct path is always directly ahead of you. Develop your own questions and processes for learning more and more about yourself. There is no one book that is a summation of your amazing and brilliant leadership. There is no one list of specific questions and answers that will ever identify everything concerning your complicated and precious life. You must self-liberate the anecdote for leadership and stop wandering in the "wilderness of leadership." You must keep your eyes open, and your aim focused.

 Enlightened with quantum knowledge of yourself, you are now ready to start the journey to becoming the absolute best leader you can possibly become. Realize this is not the final destination, but the beginning of leadership greatness. You may have spent your entire career isolated from your true leadership nature wandering in the "wilderness of your leadership." Therefore, a journey is necessary to get to the promised greatness you seek. In this promised greatness of your self-enlightened leadership, your teammates will start to understand you more because you will be able to assist them in their understanding. Your colleagues will start to understand you more because you will be able to assist them in understanding your leadership perceptions. But most of all, you will understand yourself. You will be prepared to recognize whether your talents and abilities align with your ambitions and passions for greatness. You will have a reference point for your leadership. You will be able to log on to your virtual universe, access the search engine of your leadership purpose, enter your starting point, and get accurate directions to your desired destination of greatness and maximum performance. You will have discovered who you are, and you will know exactly what you see. And that's exactly where you want to be—on the path to leadership greatness.

Your leadership greatness must allow you to connect the lines between your perceptions, values, and interests, as well as those of your staff, if you expect unprecedented levels of success and high achievement in leadership performance. Remember, you must do the work of discovering who you are, learning how you see the world, and determining how to integrate the views and opinions of others into your every leadership decision. This is the essence of exceptional leadership. The process of self-discovery is not the finish line; it's the starting point, the very crux from which every exceptional leader grows. So, again, ask yourself if your current leadership model allows you to travel every inch of your organization and provides for self-discovery and other-people centeredness along the way. Are you where you want to be as a professional? The many treacherous pathways to exceptional leadership are inundated with many challenges along the way. The weary travelers of the pathways to leadership success and high achievement must be wise enough to understand that candidates for greatness are subjugated by a series of rigorous principles that determine their success. In the spirit of the great leadership challenge, we must assess our own abilities and commitment to advance down the path of exceptional leadership and understanding our leadership psyche is critical.

> *"Direct your eyesight inward, and you'll find a thousand regions in your mind yet undiscovered. Travel them and be expert on home cosmography."*
> —Henry David Thoreau

A leadership perceptual psyche, also called leadership perceptual expectancy or just leadership psyche is a human psychological predisposition to perceive leadership with the senses in a unique manner. It is an example of how a leader's perception can be shaped by hierarchal processes that create individual drive and expectation. Perceptual psyches occur differently in all the different senses. They can be long term, such as a special sensitivity to hearing one's own child's name yelled in a crowded room, or short term, as in the case with which people who are fasting more intensely notice the smell of food. A leadership perceptual psyche can be created by personal motivation and can also result in people interpreting ambiguous figures so that they see what they choose to see. Remember, it is not what you are looking at, but what you see. And we all see things differently. For instance, how someone perceives the accuracy of an official's call in a sports game can be biased if one has a favorite team they are cheering for. In another instance, employees are allocated pleasant or unpleasant tasks by a supervisor. They respond to the tasks according to their perceptual psyche toward the tasks. Pleasant tasks are approached with excitement and high expectations. Unpleasant tasks are looked upon with contempt. Who we are and what we see matters the most.

A leader's perceptual psyche is demonstrated in many leadership contexts. Leaders who are perceived as "warm" are more likely to be perceived in a variety of positive characteristics in relation to their leadership. If the word "warm" is replaced with "incapable," then the leader will be perceived in more negative terms. When a leader has a reputation for being intelligent, he or she is more likely to find himself or herself leading people who believe in their abilities. Individuals' perceptual psyche reflects their personality traits, values, interests, and perceptions. For example, employees with lazy personality traits are quicker to correctly identify with lethargic words or situations. One classic psychological experiment showed slower work performance when employees labeled as lazy are subjected to low levels of office lighting in the workplace.

A Leadership Performance Perspective: The reality in the workplace is that employees seek out personalities that are the most conducive to their individual personality traits. Employees align with leaders that support their perceptual psyche. High-performing leaders attract the attention of high-performing subordinates, while low-performing employees avoid coming into contact with leaders that demand and inspire high performance. As a senior executive,

I find myself supplementing the perceptual psyche of my senior leaders in an effort to create a workplace environment in which every employee feels valued. Far too many leaders today lead in isolation. They fail to connect their individual perceptual psyche with the perceptual psyche of their line staff. As a result, many employees feel undervalued and underappreciated in the workplace. Leadership greatness can be measured by the degree to which every employee feels valued and appreciated. This is the very reason that understanding perceptual psyche in leadership is so critical to creating winning workplace environments and high-performing teams.

Exercise: *Complete the following actions to help in understanding just how the differences in perspective can impact your leadership behaviors.*

Ask your employees to describe your personality traits.
Ask your colleagues to describe your personality traits.
Describe the personality traits of your direct reports.
Describe the personality traits of your colleagues.
Identify the employees that align with your personality traits.
Identify the employees that do not align with your personality traits.

As you travel down your path toward exceptional leadership, discovered and perceptual, expend a tremendous amount of energy in the self-care and self-development of your leadership perceptual psyche. Always know who you are. Develop a maintenance program that assists you in remaining completely self-aware because your perceptions, beliefs, and values should and will change over time. Exercise your leadership, connect with the perceptual psyche of others, and drive your organization to higher levels of performance through motivation and expectations constructed at the molecular level of human psychology. Who we are matters. What we see matters the most. The exceptional leader understands that perceptions are the very lines of connection that predetermine whether the journey is possible. When you give such personal attention to yourself and others, you energize and incite yourself to serve others and inspire them to follow you. If no one is following, you are not a leader. *Greatness Is What Greatness Does.* Are you ready to become an exceptional leader? Perception, understanding that who you are matters, is the first principle you must master along the way.

PRINCIPLE TWO

Relationships

Relationships: Exceptional Relationships are the bedrocks of exceptional leadership.

> *"To become a great leader, you must build great relationships. Birthright may make you a King, but only great relationships can make you a Great King. Your relationships are the very foundation upon which you lift yourself above your limits, beyond your goals, and toward your successes."*
>
> —Ronald T. Hickey

Everyone has the ability to achieve greatness. Each person has their own level of success. The primary reason one does not reach greatness is because humans tend to chase the greatness of others and not their individual greatness. We must understand that one's life is not another's life. One's greatness is not another's greatness. As Americans, we have made the pursuit of money our highest priority in this country. We tend to forego quality, highly principled, human relationships for the sake of getting rich. Exceptional leadership must restore to the American fabric a common thread that demands greatness once again. Leadership must bestow upon the American workforce a greater sense of who we are and what we are still capable of. Getting rich cannot remain our most lofty pursuit if we are to remain the beacon on the hill of greatness in humanity. To do

PRINCIPLE TWO: RELATIONSHIPS

anything strictly to make money is to lose your soul and risk the lives of your followers. When creating quality relationships with other humans becomes our most cherished aim in life, then, and only then, will we advance greatly on the path upward in all American industries and interests. The country is marred in a valley of mediocrity. Only great leadership, with the ability to build great relationships in our varied institutions, will succeed at lifting the country out of its valley of "good enough" and push it toward its outer extremities of greatness. While our great ambition to "become great again" may be our guiding charge, great leaders who can build great relationships must lead the way—above our limits, beyond our goals, and toward our successes. Ambition may create a strong desire to achieve something, but it is quality relationships that exist as the bedrock upon which the foundation of great success is built. Great leaders are those who can harness a great ambition to construct great relationships if he or she is to achieve high levels of success in the workplace.

To have a wonderful marriage, a couple must possess an ambition congenial to producing such a wonderful relationship. Organizational teams, like two individuals in a marriage, are formed for the purpose of achieving some common goal. So, teams in our places of commerce and in our many institutions of enterprise and public service must have leaders that can create great relationships if they are to become great teams. In fact, a relationship must exist for leadership to exist, just as a marriage requires two individuals to be in a relationship. You cannot have one without the other. There is no leadership if there is no relationship. Relationships form the basis of leadership. Relationships define the leader. A leader who builds quality relationships is defined as a great leader. A leader who builds poor relationships is defined as a poor leader, and everyone on a winning team must be in a quality relationship with the exceptional leader. An exceptional leader must know her great ambitions and the great ambitions of everyone on her team before she can inspire a common pursuit among the team members. Those collective ambitions of the individual team members must be in proper alignment, which forms the basis of the working relationship. In a business relationship, a partnership cannot survive if one partner desires fervently to become a great provider of quality public goods and the other has only a high aspiration of making money regardless of quality. The ambition to get rich is not necessarily properly aligned with the ambition of producing a quality product. The misalignment of ambition does not provide for a quality relationship to produce quality goods. John D. Rockefeller expressed, "*The person who starts out simply with the idea of getting rich won't succeed; you must have a larger ambition. There is no mystery in business. If you do each day's task successfully and stay faithfully within these natural operations of commercial laws which I talk so much about, and keep your head clear, you will come out all right.*" I think everyone would agree that John D. Rockefeller came out all right. Rockefeller also shared his ambitions to be a great leader for his team. His teammates shared their ambitions with Rockefeller. Their collective ambitions were properly aligned. As a result, the founder of Exxon Oil, John D. Rockefeller, did more than just come out all right; he became mastodonic as a businessman because he forged great relationships, which is the bedrock of a successful enterprise.

The relationship between the team leader and the team players helps establish an atmosphere for trusting teamwork and achieving success. This charitable relationship also allows the team to assess whether there is a common purpose among the team that is in complete alignment with the ambitions of the individuals and the visions of the leader. In essence, relationships determine if there truly is a team. Teammates must have a relationship in which they share common goals and interests in reaching the shared pursuit to be successful as a team. Quality relationships allow the sharing of individual ambitions with others. This involves being completely and openly honest about the high value you place on yourself and your goals in life. This is exactly what defines a relationship, but it's the responsibility that creates the relationship. Leadership is a level of responsibility not a position of power and privilege. The responsibility to parent a child creates the parent–child relationship. The responsibility to manage a group of employees creates the manager–employee relationship.

The first principle discussed the importance of *knowing who you are and understanding that what you see is the most important aspect of leadership.* Self-knowledge unlocks the mysteries of what you truly desire to do in your leadership role. Knowing your role is knowing your responsibilities as a leader, and knowing your responsibilities gives you knowledge of the relationships you must build. You are not placing a high value on your organization or your leadership if your actions support a prevarication of your true leadership responsibilities. You must have the courage and willingness to be honest about who you are as a person and about what you truly desire to become or accomplish in your leadership. You must be able to convey your true responsibilities to those you engage in relation to your leadership. You do yourself and your organization a disservice when you downplay the importance of relationships to your leadership success. Don't downplay the importance of quality relationships to your organization's success. Let everyone inside your relationships—your spouse, coworkers, bosses, friends, siblings, children, business partners, or others in your associations—know that something inside you vehemently motivates you to strive for high achievements and great successes. Build quality relationships, and you will be a great leader. Build exceptional relationships, and you will be an exceptional leader. Let everyone know you have big dreams and that you plan to devote your life to fulfilling those big dreams. If others on your team, in your personal relationships, or in your work environment fail to share your ambitions, do not support the falsehood that the endeavor will be successful, regardless of how little the possible misalignment of ambitions might be. Without common or at least complementing ambitions, teammates will be hard pressed to identify common goals and interests. Without those common goals and interests, I believe success to any degree is next to impossible. Relationships are the apparatus with which we flesh out these critical issues. If you and your spouse have competing ambitions that fail to provide for any common goals or interests, then you will develop a horrid resentment for your spouse, and your relationship will never blossom into anything special. Your marriage will eventually fail. The relationship will experience an unhealthy demise because there is no common interest upon which to focus your efforts; thus, you will simply grow apart. Likewise, if you and your teammates, at work in your organization, company, or institution, have misaligned ambitions that fail to produce common goals and interests, then you will create a work atmosphere rot with low morale, discord, and dissention within the team. Your poor relationships will define your poor leadership. Such an atmosphere is not suitable for producing an environment for great success. If such relationship conditions exist, you will eventually fail as a leader. Performance is a function of leadership; leadership is a function of relationships.

A Leadership Performance Perspective: Finding the right team to lead and the right environment to lead in is the appropriate thing to do if you plan to be highly successful, but simply changing geography very seldom places you on the right team. After a while, you discover that similar issues exist in the new situation. One of the problems with leaving one team for another, whether in personal relationships or professional settings, is that you more often than not fail to understand the reasons you were not successful in the last team. You bring your old, poor relationship-building habits into a new set of circumstances. You are clueless to the fact that not focusing on building quality relationships will hinder you in your new location. Having poor relationships with other humans is the primary reason leaders find themselves in unwinnable, unsuccessful, overly stressed, and unhealthy situations, conditions, and environments. Exceptional leaders must build exceptional workplace relationships to be highly successful. The quality of our relationships with other humans determines the quality of our success in every human endeavor. Every leader must fully understand the goals and aspirations of those they lead and form quality relationships in respect of those common interests. The relationship must form a partnership between common interests and inspired goals that simultaneously supports the desires of the individuals and the goals of the leader. There is an old Hungarian saying that "You can't ride two horses with one ass." In partnerships, there must be one vision shared by all. Two people must be in concert with one another to be successful. A husband and wife, joined as one, cannot chase separate dreams that do not provide a common thread for weaving the fabric of a great marriage. Teammates must share a common goal of winning championships if they expect to be successful. Teams simply must have a common interest that is shared by each and every person. Partnerships cannot succeed with everyone doing their own thing and promoting their individual self-interests. Quality relationships are the threads that bind us all together so we can chase lofty pursuits as teammates. The leader's highest priority is to ensure that he or she creates the atmosphere for the development and growth of quality relationships, and everyone must be in pursuit of the same goals… everyone riding the same horse.

"If you don't love them, you can't lead them."
—Eric Shinseki, Former U.S. Secretary of Veteran Affairs

Like exceptional leaders, exceptional relationships do not occur by accident. Great organizations do not develop through osmosis but because of great leaders that build great relationships. Every company has great ideas and smart people, but it takes more than great ideas and smart people to build highly successful teams. Every professional sports team has great players, great coaches, and great ambition. But great championship sports teams don't just happen. All great teams, at home, work, or play, operate within a team environment and organizational modality that provide for each member of the team feeling that the leader cares for them and loves them. Eric Shinseki, in his quote above, stressed that love is a must, the type of love that makes everyone feel cared for. Shinseki believed that if you don't care for those that you lead, then there is no foundation upon which success can be built. He believed that without love, all you have is command, and command is not quality leadership. Without love, all you have are people working simply for the paycheck. The owner of a professional sports team with an ambition of erecting a great championship franchise requires players committed to and ambitious about winning championships, not players simply obsessed with an idea of getting rich. Company CEOs, presidents, administrators, and owners with ambitions of building great organizations and companies require employees at all levels that are enamored with staunch commitment and ambitions congenial to the overall vision of the organization, not employees simply motivated by the paycheck at the end of the week or the bonuses at the end of the year. Do you remember Enron? Enron was such a company with too many employees motivated by weekly paychecks and annual bonuses. An employee who feels the company cares about them will also yearn for a great working relationship with his or her colleagues or co-workers. This provides for an atmosphere of high morale and high-performing teams. It is the responsibility of the senior leaders to give everyone a great sense of love, care, and security. When employees feel loved by upper management, they go the extra mile to ensure the company is successful." Dr. Dobbs adds, "Employees who do not feel the company cares about them develop a feeling of low worth and develop poor work habits. They become unhappy at work, their performance decreases, and their poor attendance record disenfranchises company productivity. Soon thereafter, they start to look for employment elsewhere, somewhere where they believe they can be happy.

Great leaders must develop creature habits today that will ensure they will always be able to create workplace atmospheres in which employees feel loved, cared for, and secure.

It is that very level of relationship building that wins Super Bowls, World Series, Stanley Cups, NBA Champions, and World Cups. It will also help create winning teams within your organization. I recall when I worked for Tyco International. I traveled with a group of colleagues out of Menlo Park, California, to one of our manufacturing plants in Narita, Japan, about 45 minutes by train ride outside of Tokyo. Our goal was to determine why the Japanese team was outperforming the team in Menlo Park. We discovered that the equipment, processes, and employees in both teams were not much different. There were no significant operational differences that could be identified as the reason the Japanese production outperformed the American production. One day, the plant manager abruptly ran out during a meeting. I was curious as to what had given rise to the urgency, so I followed him as quickly as I could. When I caught up with him, I found the plant manager at the exterior entrance and exit door of the building shaking every employee's hand and thanking them for their hard work as each employee left or thanking them for coming to work. Every employee waited patiently in line just so they could shake the plant manager's hand and receive his gesture of love and care. I exclaimed, "WOW!!" If you love them, you can lead them. Because the plant manager made shaking every employee's hand a priority, the employees left work or came to work feeling valued. Their feeling valued was evidenced in their productivity. I immediately understood that employees back home in Menlo Park were not shown appreciation from senior management. We had the attitude that the paycheck was enough. We did not love them in Menlo Park, so we could not lead them as employees were being led in Japan.

PRINCIPLE TWO: RELATIONSHIPS

The image below illustrates the results of building relationships of love and care.

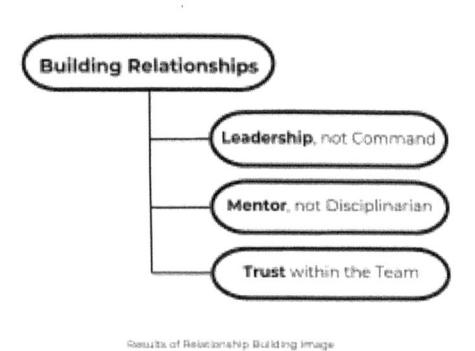

```
Building Relationships
    ├── Leadership, not Command
    ├── Mentor, not Disciplinarian
    └── Trust within the Team
```

Results of Relationship Building Image

Quality relationships provide a great leader with some extremely valuable tools for building winning teams. Those tools are leadership, mentorship, and trust.

Leadership allows the leader to operate out of a love and caring ethic. It gives the leader more than just command over subordinates, but rather a greater appeal to the nature of humans. No one enjoys being told what to do all the time. People at home and at work respect collaboration, desire partnerships, and respond to great leadership. Outside of military and paramilitary (law enforcement) contexts, command has very little viability to driving teams to high levels of performance. Command is not a function of love or appeal to the true nature of humanity. It is a "do what I say or else" sort of proposition. Command has its place in life, but not in the American workplace if building highly successful teams is your goal. The exceptional leader leads with love, respect, and common goals. Exceptional leadership builds consensus and works in collaboration.

Command commandeers the actions of others with the threat of unfavorable conditions, such as discipline. Relationships build others up; therefore, it is a tool of great leadership.

Mentorship is the companion to *Leadership*. Mentorship is the alternative to discipline. Great leaders who can mentor others create a pipeline of great leaders and eliminate the need to be a disciplinarian who drives artificial actions with arbitrary goals. With mentorship, *Greatness Is What Greatness Does*. Mentorship is the example and witness to the actions that lead great organizations to accomplish great things. Every exceptional leader aspires to mentorship not discipline.

Trust is a common goal in all relationships; without trust, no relationship is healthy. If relationships are truly the bedrock to great leadership, then trust is the cornerstone of quality relationships. Everyone wishes to follow a leader that they can trust. No one vies for a relationship with someone they do not trust. In every survey ever conducted on the quality most sought after in a leader, trust is always one of the most sought-after attributes in a leader. While Eric Shinseki says, "You can't lead them if you don't love them," I say, "You cannot lead them if they do not trust you."

A Leadership Development Perspective: While there are varied reasons employees leave an organization, the lack of trust in leadership is the #1 reason employees identify as their reason for discontinuing their employment. The #2 reason employees identify is leadership not showing that they care. By deploying great leadership, providing mentorship, displaying trustworthiness, and showing employees that you care about their well-being, leaders have the amazing ability to retain experienced and high-performing employees and drive unprecedented levels of success within the organizations they lead.

PRINCIPLE TWO: RELATIONSHIPS

If morale is extremely low within the organization, it is a leadership issue. Performance is a function of leadership. Companies find it extremely challenging to retain good employees because of the lack of trust in leadership and the lack of feeling valued. The work environment and employee morale are the responsibility of leadership in partnership with HR. Try shaking employees' hands every day to have an impact on morale in your organization. It will surely become a "WOW" moment. The handshake goes a long way in saying, "I care about your well-being as a human." Your employees will smile and thank you for caring enough to shake their hands and thank them for their hard work. Employees convey that the simple handshake makes them trust leadership and makes them feel appreciated.

With the tools of leadership, mentorship, and trust, you are ready for the next challenge. So, here is the relationship principle challenge:

The Relationship Principle Challenge:
Relationship Exercise

1. List five things you can do to build quality relationships with subordinates.
2. List five things you can do to build quality relationships with colleagues.
3. List five things you can do to build quality relationships with superiors.
4. List five things you can do to show employees that you care about them.
5. Commit to shaking every employee's hand at work every day and thank them for being a great employee of the organization.

Relationships are such an integral element to identifying your leadership ambitions. The above exercises are practically impossible to complete if you have no self-awareness or self-understanding of your ability to build quality relationships. Relationships allow a leader to identify which individuals the leader wants to build a winning championship team with. Through quality relationships, you build your championship team. Your true talents, brilliance, intelligence, and capabilities are barometers for what you have the innate ability to do. Relationships assist you in identifying your ability to partner your talents, brilliance, intelligence, and capabilities with others in a common cause.

"First say what you would be and then do what you have to."
—Epictetus

You may find your leadership is experiencing some level of disengagement, disinterest, disdain, and/or discord now or in the future. If so, be willing to accept the fact that any combination of the *4Ds of Dissatisfaction* in your team environment will severely cripple your ability to be successful as a leader or to drive your team to high levels of job performance. Creating quality relationships in the workplace brings resolve to the *4Ds of Dissatisfaction*. Quality relationships in the workplace will also produce what I label the *12 Essential Characteristics of High-Performing Teams*.

- **Trust**
  If you can't trust your teammates, you can't be in a productive relationship with them. Without trust, team members live a life of worry and doubt. No one wants to spend their workdays with the constant worry and looking over their

back that comes with distrust. It's no way to live. Trust can be a goal. It can be something the team works on and gets better at over time. So, sometimes a lack of trust (especially in the beginning) doesn't mean the team will not succeed. But you must get there at some point—if you expect to be highly successful.

- *Respect*

  Everyone wants to be respected for who they are and for what they believe they bring to the team. Everyone has a degree of talent, intellect, and ability that lends itself to the team's success. If a person does not feel respected for their abilities, then they can never feel comfortable on the team. Respect provides a comfort level that eliminates the feeling of vulnerability. Quality relationships in the workplace eliminate any sense of vulnerability.

- *Safety and Security*

  Safety and security are the first level on Maslow's human behavior pyramid. Everyone must feel safe and secure to remain interested in being a part of any team. If a team cannot make its member feel a great sense of safety and security, then teammates will not stick around. This is a basic human need. Quality relationships will ensure that everyone feels safe and secure.

- *Happiness*

  Everyone wants to be happy with their job and with those they work with. Happiness is essential. While no one is happy all the time, happiness cannot be a fleeting aspect of the team environment. An unhappy team member is an underperforming team member. When employees add up the total of happy times versus unhappy times, happy times must come out on top. Otherwise, people develop low morale and start looking to leave the company. Quality relationships promote happiness in the workplace.

- *A Sense of Belonging*

  All humans tend to harbor a sense of wanting to belong to something greater than themselves. Everyone strives for some degree of greatness and belonging to a team that accepts them for who they are and for what value they bring to the teams. People take great pride in great accomplishments. We want to wear the paraphernalia that identifies us as members of our championship teams. Quality relationships welcome team members into the fraternity.

- **Quality Communication**

  Communication is what fuels relationships and drives the success of the best teams. I don't believe that there can be real, lasting relationships of any sort without good communication. *You need quality communication in workplace relationships* to set expectations, express your goals, fix problems, express your needs, and even to have good professional interactions. Communication is essentially everything. So, if you're with teammates you can't communicate with or don't communicate well with, you must be able to fix that, for no amount of money will produce the happy, healthy relationship needed to be highly successful. Quality communication is essential to quality relationships.

- **High Morale**

  If communication is the fuel, then morale is the heartbeat of the relationship. Morale is how a person feels about themselves in association with the team. High morale produces high-performing teams. Low morale produces low-performing teams. No one wants to be in a team

PRINCIPLE TWO: RELATIONSHIPS

environment drowning in low morale. Quality relationships are critical to the team's morale.

- *A Sense of Self*

    Everyone is an "individual" before they become part of a team. We have all heard that there is no "I" in "Team." But everyone wants to maintain their individual identity, even when on a team. There's no team great enough to give up one's self-identity for. No one should be required to give up the essence of who they are; after all, who you are matters. If you get into a relationship and *you ultimately lose yourself*, you forget your interests, you give up on your goals, and you just aren't the person you want to be—that's a problem. No amount of success is worth giving up the fundamental truths of who you are. Quality relationships respect the individual's need to self-identify with their individual truths.

- *Comradery*

    Teammates must get along with each other. Otherwise, dissention, hatred, jealousy, resentfulness, and discord take center stage. But it's more common than you think for people to stay in working relationships with people they don't actually like because they need the money. Teammates who are in it just for the money are not team players and normally are the biggest underperformers who bring the team's performance down. Quality relationships ensure everyone gets along with each other on the team.

- *A Sense of Freedom*

    A person must be free to function at their absolute best. Being free to do the things you want to do, to be yourself, to go places, to *have your own thoughts and feelings*, and to have a say in how your life goes is not just important in a workplace relationship; it is essential. A sense of independence by the individual is an essential characteristic of high-performing teams. You must have a sense that you can think critically and use your amazing imagination. You can (and often should) include your teammates in collaboration with your decisions, but you should still feel free to think critically. Is the working relationship really worth it if you feel like you have to ask for permission to be yourself or if your team will not allow you do what you do best? Quality relationships allow you to be your best.

- *Partnership*

    Quality relationships are about the quality of the partnerships that drive teams to be high-performing teams. In a true partnership, everyone knows and accepts their role and executes without delay or disdain for others. If there are no partnerships among the teammates, then there is essentially no team. Relationships, by their sheer nature, are partnerships. The degree to which the partnership performs depends majorly on the quality of the relationship among the members.

- *Self-Actualization*

    Often, working in team environments can be totally complicated. You can love your work but not your teammates. You must see yourself, your successes, and your self-guided motivation to be successful. Self-actualization is the highest point on Maslow's human behavior pyramid. You might have other goals, you might feel emotionally unstable, or you might just not be *ready to make a commitment*. If so, you are not self-actualized and could hurt the team's performance. Timing is important here, too. You must want to be in a team relationship. Quality relationships create the

PRINCIPLE TWO: RELATIONSHIPS

desire to want to be on the team and give you that strong sense of self-actualization.

All work relationships in the team environment are different, and many problems are solvable with a focus on creating quality relationships with the *12 Essential Characteristics of Highly Performing Teams* in mind. These 12 characteristics are not the only ingredients in quality relationships but are (arguably) the most important ingredients in a healthy workplace relationship.

> *"If you aspire to be the most amazing leader on earth, you need to be ambitious enough to build the most amazing relationships on earth."*
>
> —Ronald T. Hickey

A woman once wrote, "*A woman who aspires to be equal with men lacks ambition.*" Identifying your ambitions and the relationships required to produce the level of success you seek is very critical to your becoming an exceptional leader. Equally essential to the ultimate manifestation of your greatness is the understanding of the true and quintessential power of ambitious relationship building. Remember, ambition raises us above ourselves, above our failures, above our obstacles, and above our limits. Ambitious relationships are the driving force that pushes us forward when everything in our lives tells us we cannot succeed. Ambitious relationships are the life form that creates an unyielding desire in a man to become the president of the United States of America, despite the fact that he was raised by a single White mother after his African father abandoned them when he was only 2 years old. Ambition orders the steps of a little girl born and raised in an impoverish trailer park and takes her to the stage of a theatre where she accepts the Academy Award for Best Actress. Ambition creates relationships. Ambition has no limits. It will deliver you to any destination you choose. Do you want to be a great leader of a great team? If so, be ambitious enough to create the necessary relationships. Do you want to be promoted to the CEO of your company? Then be ambitious enough to do so and create the necessary relationships. *Greatness Is What Greatness Does*. And greatness builds great relationships. Do you want to become as great as you want to be? All you need to do is understand the true power of relationships; if you doubt its true power in the slightest, you may want to consider what it has allowed Barack Obama, Hillary Swank, Jamie Foxx, Steve Jobs, Joel Osteen, T.D. Jakes, Larry King, Kobe Bryant, LeBron James, Jeff Bezos, Serena Williams, Tiger Woods, and so many others to accomplish in their lives. Ambition has the power to do the same for you. Identify your ambitions and the ambitions of others. Your greatness depends on you doing so!

A Leadership Performance Perspective: Great leaders are ever pressed to make a bold determination to follow their leadership intuitions at a moment's notice. Your leadership skill in relationship building must be partnered with an undying passion to lead and succeed in intense situations and challenging times. Passion is a fiery love. You must passionately love what you do. To be great at anything, you must have a passion for it. Your passion causes you to love what you do so much that it sets your soul on fire.

A good friend of mine played at the highest level in the NFL for 10 years. He said his soul was on fire every day he played the game. He told me that he had an undying passion for the game and for being the best player he could possibly be. In leadership, as in sports, your passion will fuel your purpose. There must be a strong relationship between your passion and purpose. Your purpose must be the greatness motivation in your leadership. One must also be willing to pass the fire on to others. That's really what relationships are all about—passing your fire on to the next person. The followers of your leadership will label you an exceptional leader when you commit to building quality relationships and infecting others on your team with your passion. This is exactly why we are able to build a great team of high performers. Exceptional leaders must always be aware of everything happening around them; especially aware of the quality of the relationships within their immediacy. Auspicious evidence of quality relationships, while not always easily detected, conveys that exceptional leaders are positioned for high levels of success. Quality relationships will help you resist the temptation to move hastily. Quality relationships will allow you to take time to enjoy the moment in front of you, shake hands, and build trust. Leaders are human and must develop the innate ability to enjoy the resolve of their hearts, the boldness of their steps, the power of their expectations, the sanguinity of their drive, and the faith in their abilities. Great human relationships make you feel this way. Nothing outside and beyond the valuable relationships you build should matter more to your success as a leader. Without quality relationships, there can be no great leadership. In the condition of solitude and vulnerability, you must navigate the challenges of your leadership's pursuit down the pathway to greatness. You alone must vow to make something great of your leadership. No one can do it for you; others can only help you based on the quality of the relationships you have given birth to. There is a transformative effect to building quality relationships that affords your leadership an amazing tool for engaging your followers at the highest plateau of team performance. With this commitment and the principle of creating quality relationships, you will place your organization on a trajectory of unprecedented success. Your unwavering commitment to your leadership greatness will give birth to your success. Your teammates, employees, colleagues, and superiors will trust you and feel appreciated by your leadership, and you are now ready to win championships, for *Greatness Is What Greatness Does*.

PRINCIPLE THREE

Inspiration

Inspiration: An Exceptional Leader inspires a shared vision.

"Inspiration can be an insatiable and implacable passion. But understand that inspiration alone will never guarantee success. All the inspiration in the world will not help you catch a fish if there are no fish in the water."
—Ronald T. Hickey

Every exceptional leader is inspired to be exceptional. Inspiration creates a strong desire to achieve greatly in some endeavor. As a great leader, you must harness great inspiration if you are to achieve great success. To produce a championship caliber organization, everyone on the team must possess an inspiration that is impassioned to produce such an organization. Teams in the workplace, like teams anywhere, are formed for the purpose of achieving something great and something in common. So, teams must have great inspiration if they are to become great teams and win championships. The leader is responsible for inspiring greatness, a shared vision, and common goals. Everyone on the team must be inspired and aligned with the vision and goals of the leader. The exceptional leader must be able to inspire others to share in his or her vision if the team is to achieve greatness in everything the team endeavors to accomplish. The team's shared vision, common goals, and collective inspirations must be in proper alignment with the organizational objectives, values, and mission.

Inspiring others involves being completely and openly honest about the high value you place on yourself and your goals in life and in the organization. The last chapter discussed the exceptional leadership principle of *building quality relationships*. The relationship between your personal goals and your professional goals unlocks the mysteries of what you truly desire to do with your life and your leadership. You are not placing a high value on your true self if your actions support a prevarication of your true inspirations. You must have the courage and willingness to be honest about who you are as a person and about what you truly desire to become or accomplish in your leadership. You do yourself and others a disservice when you play yourself small. Don't play yourself small; *Greatness Is What Greatness Does*. If you are inspired to be great, you will do great things. Inspiration is the third principle of exceptional leadership. Does everyone around you know what you are inspired to accomplish? Be transparent and forthright with your inspiration. Let everyone—your spouse, co-workers, superiors, board of directors, friends, siblings, children, business partners, and others in your associations—know that something inside you vehemently motivates you to strive for high achievements and great successes. When others see what you are inspired to accomplish, they will follow. Let everyone know you have big dreams and that you plan to devote your life to fulfilling those big dreams. If others on your team, in your personal relationships, or in your work environment share your inspirations, you are on your way to leading yourself and others to great success, and inspiration will fuel the journey. Without inspired common goals, a common vision, or an inspiration for greatness, what can a team accomplish?

A Leadership Performance Perspective: *If you and your staff have competing visions and goals that fail to provide inspiration to struggle through the challenges in the workplace, then you will develop a horrid resentment for your coworkers, and your performance will never blossom into anything special. More than likely, any attempt at building a successful team will experience an unhealthy demise because there are no common interests upon which to focus your efforts; thus, you will simply complete work tasks that are disconnected from any productive goals. Likewise, if you and your teammates at work have misaligned inspirations that fail to produce common goals and interests, then you will create an atmosphere rot with low morale, discord, and dissention within the team. Such an atmosphere is not suitable for providing an opportunity for success. If such conditions exist and circumstances allow, you as the leader in your organization are charged with the responsibility of inspiring a common vision and common goals among the staff. You cannot lead people to greatness if you cannot inspire a common goal.*

Does your leadership inspire greatness? While inspiring others can be a challenging task, the ability to inspire others separates exceptional leaders from mediocre leaders. Ask yourself, "What exactly do I inspire in others?" Whether there are two, three, four, five, or 5,000 people in an organization, everyone must be in concert with one another to be exceptionally successful. As mentioned in the previous chapter, a husband and wife, joined as one, cannot chase separate dreams that do not provide a common thread for weaving the fabric of a great marriage. Teammates must share a common goal of winning championships if they expect to be successful. Teams simply must have a common interest that is shared by each and every member. Partnerships cannot succeed with everyone doing their own thing and promoting their individual self-interests. An exceptional leader is one who can inspire such a shared vision and common interests that produce high performance.

> *"Keep away from people who try to belittle your ambitions. Small people do that, but the really great make you feel that you, too, can become great."*
>
> —Mark Twain

It is worth repeating that great leadership does not occur by accident. Great organizations do not develop through osmosis. Great victories do not just happen. All great accomplishments, at home, work, or play, operate within a team environment and modality that provide for each member of the team identifying and sharing their inspirations. When properly inspired, a team will ask honest questions of itself. The team asks questions to determine if there are common goals and interests among all the teammates. The team asks questions to assess if there is a commitment to achieving something great. The owner of a professional sports team with an inspiration of erecting a great championship franchise requires players committed to and ambitious about winning championships, not players simply obsessed with an idea of getting rich. This goes right back to what John D. Rockefeller was quoted as saying in the second principle. Company CEOs, presidents, administrators, leaders, and owners with ambitions of building great organizations and companies require employees at all levels that are armed with commitment and inspirations in complete support of the overall vision of the organization, not employees simply motivated by the paycheck at the end of the week or the bonuses at the end of the year. Remember, Enron was such a company with too many employees motivated by weekly paychecks and annual bonuses. An organization that yearns for greatness requires a group of professionals committed and inspired to be exceptional, not colleagues simply onboard the ship for self-serving reasons such as bonuses, power, or greed. In any of your situations, either at home, work, or play, you must ask questions to ascertain whether you are truly inspired in a situation that will provide you the environment in which great accomplishments will be achieved by your version of inspiration. You must have those tough conversations about the shared and common inspirations of everyone involved. You must understand whether you, as the leader, can inspire your team, with their varying perceptions and relationships, to greatness.

A Leadership Development Perspective: *Develop workplace habits today that will ensure you will always have the ability to identify the alignment of your inspirations with the inspirations of those on your team. If your inspirations and those of your teammates or subordinates do not align, have the professional fortitude and courage to have open dialogue and determine whether proper alignment can be achieved toward the common goal of exceptionalism. And if you determine that proper alignment is possible and worth the leadership effort, play yourself "BIG" (Brilliant–Inspirational–Great) and inspire your team or organization to greatness. Listen to John D. Rockefeller and don't hang around simply for the paycheck. Give up the good and go be as great as you can be. Always, always, always play yourself "BIG!" Inspire others beyond themselves, beyond their limits, beyond their failures, and over their obstacles.*

So, here is the inspiration challenge: Identify your inspirations so you can always play yourself as a "BIG" leader at work and on your teams. Review your responses to the exercises in Principle 2 and then answer the following questions:

The Inspiration Challenge:
First Exercise
What inspires you to be a leader?
What does your leadership inspire others to achieve?
What makes you a great leader?
List the shared vision, common goals, and interests you inspire?
What prevents you from playing yourself "BIG" in your leadership role?
Now review the answers from the challenges in Principle 1 and complete the following:

Second Exercise
Identify your personal inspirations.
Identify the personal inspirations of every member of your team.
Identify 10 reasons why you believe your current team(s) provide(s) an environment that supports your inspiration to achieve greatness.
Identify 10 reasons why you believe your current team(s) *do(es) not* provide an environment that supports your inspirations to achieve greatness.
List three reasons why you believe you are the leader who can inspire every member of your current team(s).

Self-evaluation is such an integral element to identifying your inspirations. The above exercises are practically impossible to complete if you have no self-awareness or self-understanding. Self-discovery helps you to first determine what you want to be great at. Your true talents, brilliance, intelligence, and capabilities are barometers for what you have the God-given volition, talent, and ability to do. Self-discovery assists you in identifying your ability to inspire others. Are you an inspirational leader? An exceptional leader is exceptionally inspirational. Inspiration gives you the courage to say that you can accomplish when others tell you that you cannot. Inspiration tells you that whatever the endeavor requires, you will meet the challenge. Inspiration causes you to play yourself "BIG" and encourage others to be great. With courage and confidence at your sides, tell yourself just how great you want to become and then do whatever it takes. Then tell everyone around you that they can be great as well. Realize that becoming great may entail waving goodbye to your current associations and taking your "BIG" self elsewhere.

A Leadership Development Perspective: *When I realized my inspirations to become a professional leadership development consultant, organizational development consultant, and performance manager, I also realized that my place of employment did not provide the proper environment or modality for me becoming a great business consultant or great performance coach. I knew in my heart that I would have to one day say goodbye to my current team and commission another winning team if I intended to seriously pursue my desire to become what I so strongly desired. My gained leadership experience, talent, and inspirations aligned perfectly with my passion for becoming a peak performance consultant and author. My life experiences, education, and employment history had delivered me to this apex where my talents, ambition, and vision aligned properly for a career in helping others manage their personal and* *professional lives. My talents, ambition, and vision were not properly aligned with the goals and interests of others around me for high achievement and great success at my current place of employment. This misalignment of ambition and vision was the root cause of my disgruntlement with my current job situation, even though I was the senior leader. I simply was not happy with my job. So, I decided that it was finally time to do what I have always wanted to do. I knew I had to take my "BIG" self elsewhere and do whatever was required of me to become the person I wanted to be. My decision to become as great as I wanted to be is what caused me to sit down with a focused purpose and write this book that you now read. I am living proof that when you identify your ambition, become inspired by a great leader, and have the courage and confidence to follow your dreams, BIG things will happen in life. With this book, I am on a team that has a star at every position, and we share a common vision to write a book on leadership that inspires others to chase down their greatness. Greatness really is what greatness does.*

The Satisfaction Challenge:
Third Exercise

1. Pause here and seriously contemplate the current situations in your current teams. Review your answers to the questions you provided in the second exercise.
2. Now consider both exercises in their entirety. Determine whether any feelings and thoughts of disengagement, disinterest, disdain, and/or discord are due to contrasting inspirations between you and members of your team.
3. Determine, unequivocally, whether each of your current team members have ambitions, purposes, goals, and interests that align with your leadership goals.

PRINCIPLE THREE: INSPIRATION

4. Based on these determinations, make an inspiration-influenced decision for whether you are satisfied in your current leadership role. And whatever you decide, always play yourself "BIG."
5. Say you will be an exceptional leader who will inspire others to be great and then do what you need to.

A Leadership Performance Perspective: After determining that your inspirations align with all members of your team or after deciding to move to another team where inspiration and vision alignment is possible, make sure you have positioned yourself for success. Your inspirations must be coupled with attainable goals. Your inspirations and the inspirations of your organization will be in vain, no matter the level of the effort or the commitment to goals and values, if your situation provides for no possibility of success. If you are ambitious about traveling to the moon, understand that your inspiration alone will not propel you to outer space; you will need great inspiration and a damn good space rocket. If you know your ambitious endeavors will require a team of individuals to be successful, then don't go at it alone. Go recruit the top talent. Make sure there is a star at every position. One high-performing employee is 10 times more productive than the average employee. Therefore, there is a premium on top talent. Great companies require great individuals and a great support system. Great workplaces don't just happen; they are built by great leaders who assemble great teams. So many leaders go into a leadership role with an expectation of having a great working relationship with great team members, but they knowingly attempt to catch fish in waters where there are no fish. You can't catch fish in a lake that has no fish. You can't be a great leader if you don't have great people to lead. Be inspired, but also be smart. The true intelligence of a leader is demonstrated by who gets hired. Great companies require great people at all rungs of the organizational ladder, but companies, time and time again, hire people who are not qualified for the job they are hired to perform. I find it so hard to believe that companies continue to hire a person after only interviewing the person just once and for only a few minutes. How can one possibly assess vision, ambition, talent, and potential utilizing such an empty process? I recall being hired as an assistant superintendent in a public school district in the state of California and asking the hiring manager if she had googled me. She looked perplexed and stated that she had not. I asked if she had hired me based solely on my resume and my responses to 10 interview questions. She said that was precisely her process. This particular position in education was the worst employment experience of my career in education and identifies why public education can be a very challenging industry to work in. The American work environment is quickly deteriorating because so many people are misaligned with the tasks they are hired to perform. Unfortunately, people are misaligned because the hiring process is defunct in most organizations and human resources personnel are unqualified to make adequate recruitment and staffing decisions. A star company requires stars that are properly aligned at every position, especially in the leadership positions.

We make similar decisions in our personal lives as well. I know several individuals who decided to marry after having known the other person only a few months. That process speaks volumes about the two individuals involved and their commitment to having a great relationship. Many years are typically required before the universe reveals to a person their true purpose, vision, and inspirations in life. The universe allows us to mature our minds and develop our talents. We make many changes in life along the way. And when we are ready to accept our true purpose, the lifelong pursuit that will make us

PRINCIPLE THREE: INSPIRATION

happy beyond our wildest dreams, God brings us into complete alignment with the things required for the journey to greatness. This alignment is a time-consuming process that cannot be circumvented. Circumventing universal laws leads to destitution, despair, and the 4Ds of dissatisfaction. Look at every individual who married the wrong person at the wrong time. Look at every organization with mediocre employees at every level hired too quickly just because some human resources specialist is driven by the rate at which they can close out the job requisitions in their files. Almost every job I have ever held has required me to work with individuals who were not even remotely qualified to do the jobs they were hired to perform. This identifies a failure of the human resources function that needs to get better in every organization.

When you apply for a job with an organization and are fortunate enough to be invited to interview for a position, become intimate with the process. Realize that the process you are subjected to will be similar to the process utilized for selecting everyone you will be required to work with. Learn to desire and appreciate a rigorous hiring process that is truly modeled for finding and selecting the best person for the position. The best person will be a high-performing star. An exceptional leader attracts, hires, and inspires top talent. If you feel the process was sufficient for determining your talent, inspiration, and vision, then there can be an expectation for inspiration alignment within the organization. I have rejected employment offers made to me when I was selected after having been interviewed only once for 30 minutes. I have learned from experience that such organizations will result in job dissatisfaction for me. I am at a point in my life where I have been very successful and need more than just a paycheck. My inspirations are much loftier than simply getting rich. If you are the hiring manager, don't feel obligated to continue to fail your organization simply because the human resource function is inadequate. Develop fair and legal processes for determining if the people coming into your company have the talent, inspiration, and long-term vision that are in complete alignment with the overall vision and needs of your team. Your ability to achieve greatness depends on your leadership ability to attract the absolute best people.

When I worked for a company that produced products supporting the aerospace industry and the United States Armed Forces, I had a difficult time understanding why the company struggled to remain profitable, given the current state of world conflict on every continent on the globe. After close observation, I then realized that the company was a mediocre, at best, company because the organization hired mediocre, at best, employees at every rung of the organizational ladder. The company had no process that identified and analyzed the inspirations of potential or current employees as part of the employment selection process. We need similar assessment processes for determining the inspirations of individuals we are contemplating teaming up with, whether in our professional or personal lives. Without these processes, we potentially find ourselves fishing with the inspiration of becoming great fishers in waters where there are no fish. At this aerospace company, as with essentially every position I have held in public education, I found myself fishing in a lake that had few or no fish.

"The man who understands how something is done will always be employed. The man who understands why something is done will always be the boss of the man who only

PRINCIPLE THREE: INSPIRATION

knows how. But the woman who owns the company understands the true and ultimate power of inspiration."
—Ronald T. Hickey

A man once wrote, "*A man who aspires to be equal to another man lacks inspiration.*" Identifying your inspirations and the inspirations of others is essential to your well-being. Equally essential to the ultimate manifestation of your greatness is the understanding of the true and quintessential power of inspiration. Remember, inspiration raises us above ourselves, our failures, our obstacles, and our limits. Inspiration is the driving force that pushes us forward when everything in our lives tells us we cannot succeed. As previously stated, inspiration is the life form that creates an unyielding desire in a man or woman to become the greatness they dream of. Inspiration has the power to do the same for you. Identify your inspirations and the inspirations of others. Your greatness depends on you doing so! Say what you will do, and then do what you must.

As an exceptional leader, you have determined to follow your inspirations. Your leadership purpose has become the deepest meaning in your life. The walls of your mind reverberate the sound of your voice that shouts, "I will be a great leader!" This is the moment of your new beginning. Look around you; all auspicious evidence conveys that the universe is positioned for your orderly progression toward great success. Resist the temptation to move hastily and take time to enjoy this moment in front of you. Enjoy the resolve of your inspiration, the boldness of your vision, the innocence of your expectations, the sanguinity of your hope, and the faith of your team. You will never feel this way again. Now, start by deciding to commit to your inspirations you have identified. Nothing outside and beyond these inspirations should matter to you at this point. Play yourself "BIG." In this condition of solitude and vulnerability, you must navigate the challenges of your leadership pursuit down the pathway to greatness. You alone must vow to make something of your leadership. No one can do it for you. There is a transformative effect to this knowledge that renders your soul the very tool for engaging the workplace on this highest plateau of leadership atonement. With this commitment to exceptional leadership, the universe has set in route to your location everything you require to become great. The favorable signs that are now so vivid to you bear witness to this response of the universe. Your unwavering commitment to your inspirations and your ability to inspire others will give birth to your success. Congratulations! You have taken the giant step toward becoming as great of a leader as you want to be. *Greatness Is What Greatness Does.*

A Leadership Performance Perspective: What inspirational leadership truly comes down to is the leader's ability to inspire greatness—can the leader inspire maximum performance? Maximum input produces maximum output. Maximum In—Maximum Out: MIMO. When properly inspired to give a maximum effort, we do everything we can do. Does your leadership inspire others to give their best effort in they everything do?

Maximum Leadership Performance and Development
- Measurements of Leadership Performance Indicators
  - What is your Leadership? – **Strength**
  - What is your Leadership? – **Speed**
  - What is your Leadership? – **Agility**
  - What is your Leadership? – **Endurance**
  - What is your Leadership? – **Toughness**

PRINCIPLE THREE: INSPIRATION

- Two Simple Leadership Philosophies
  - You must commit to "Maximize" what you do every day. You cannot cheat the universe, for the universe knows what you have put in—MIMO!
  - You must commit every day to improving upon what you accomplished yesterday. You must be determined to reach your destination along a delineation to better yourself every day.
- Principles of Maximum Performance
  - **Purpose:** Your purpose powers your mind.
  - **Vision:** Your vision drives your body.
  - **Passion:** Your passion fuels your soul.

Maximum performance development (MPD) is a performance development process that will help individuals develop and manage personal performance skills that will produce maximum performance and maximize productivity in individual performers, leaders, high-performing teams, and world-class winning organizations.

Measurements of Performance Indicators in the Workplace. There is an athletic aspect to everything we do in the workplace. To reach a level of greatness, one must reach a level of maximum performance, metaphorically, similar to the athletic attributes of a world-class athlete. What are your job performance measurements? Whether you are the CEO, director of human resources, department manager, division leader, supervisor, individual producer, or team player, what are your performance measurements in strength, speed, agility, endurance, and toughness?

Performance–**Strength:** What is your skill level, education, training, and experience? How can you build your performance strength?

Performance–**Speed:** How quickly, effectively, and efficiently can you get the job done? What is your performance level based on deadlines and budgets? What can you do to increase your performance speed?

Performance–**Agility:** What is your ability to adapt to evolving changes in the industry or marketplace? How flexible are your operations and your decision-making abilities? Can you create new ways of performing your job duties more effectively and efficiently? What can you do to expand your agility and become more adaptable in your job performance?

Performance–**Endurance:** Do you engage in performance workout, come in early, or stay late to increase your endurance? Do you go the extra mile and exercise your skills to ensure you have the lung capacity in your job performance to outlast the competition? What can you do to raise your workplace job performance endurance?

Performance–**Toughness:** Do you possess mental toughness for when things become challenging? When things get overwhelming, do you respond with vigor or crumble under the weight of stress? How can you increase your mental toughness in the workplace?

Exercise:

List three things you will commit to maximizing every day. Maximum In—Maximum Out!

List three things you will commit to doing better today than you did yesterday?

PRINCIPLE THREE: INSPIRATION

Exceptional leadership must inspire a common goal and a shared vision, and those visions and goals must inspire greatness. Greatness comes with a particular level of determination. Greatness is a destination as well. It has a specific line of delineation. Exceptional leadership inspires great determination, great destinations, and great delineation. Combine these amazing attributes with maximum effort in performance, and you will surely find your leadership greatness—*Greatness Is What Greatness Does.*

PRINCIPLE FOUR

NOW

NOW: A Great Leader must be in the NOW—Navigating with Organizational focus and a Worldview.

> *"An exceptional leader must be able to learn and grow from the past, lead and navigate toward the future, all while living and thriving in the NOW. An exceptional leader must be connected and engaged with every aspect of the organization. I call that being TAPPED IN!"*
> —Ronald T. Hickey

The quality of leadership is determined by the aspects of the leader's actions, focus, and perspective. To be a great leader, one must be capable of superb actions, high performance, and excellent perspective. To lead highly successful teams and organizations, a leader must, at all times, be navigating, *taking all of the appropriate actions*, with an organizational focus, *thriving for high-performing outcomes*, in pursuit of world-class excellence in the NOW. Far too often, challenging circumstances are offered for the reason a leader may not have been focused, may have made a bad decision, or may have acted outside of the mission. "I wasn't aware" is an all too familiar reframe. Stepping into challenging and deceptive leadership roles is not the reason a leader fails to rise to a level of excellence in a leadership position. A great leader must always possess the capacity to take the

PRINCIPLE FOUR: NOW

appropriate actions and unleash a perspective of excellence on the human environments within which they intend to carve out a great leadership platform. Appropriate actions, being in the NOW, can be defined by three factors: timing, awareness, and position (TAP). If we are in the right place, at the right time, and aware of the opportunity, then we are "TAPPED IN" and operating in the NOW. If we are TAPPED IN, then every action we take will be appropriate and impactful and will produce a positive outcome. Great leaders can take full advantage of situations when presented with the opportunity. If leaders are not at the right place, are not in the right time, and are unaware of the opportunity, then they cannot to act appropriately to take advantage of the opportunity that has been presented to the team or organization, and they are "tapped out." We are either TAPPED IN or tapped out in leadership, which ultimately determines the level of success, breadth of excellence, and impact on performance.

When tapped out, one may not realize that they have become stalled in a leadership dead spot—low performance of undesirable and stultifying conditions that produces subpar productivity. A leadership dead spot robs the leader of his or her leadership strength insomuch as she is neither aware of her conditions nor in a position to impact her conditions, even if time is on her side. When the workplace presents an opportunity for an increase, we must be ready to act with assuredness and intrepidness. To be a great leader, one must be focused, possess the proper perspective, and TAPPED IN at all times, and exceptional leaders must act with the purpose and vision of a great navigator. The lack of vision and purpose are the results of being tapped out. Having no purpose causes a leader to have no confidence in his or her timing and position. So, the leader is never properly prepared to achieve high levels of excellence. Lacking vision is the result of not fully recognizing the opportunity. So, the leader never achieves his or her best because the leader is never quite ready to seize the opportunities that offer greatness. As a result of no vision or purpose, leaders console themselves with the privileges of the position and accept being just good enough or mediocrity. Leadership should never be looked upon as a position of privilege but rather as the degree of responsibility to produce successful organizations and a measure of opportunity for becoming a better leader. This holds true for every leader, irrespective of current circumstances. Thus, even if you are positioned in a leadership dead spot today, tomorrow can provide the opportunity to better your situation. But you must be in the right place at the right time and able to recognize the opportunity. If you are, your actions will be appropriate, and the quality of your leadership will increase without limits.

Three decades ago, I visited the town of Tunica, Mississippi. I was traveling with Dexter Clancy, a friend I had met while serving in the United States Navy. Dexter, a man with a quiet disposition and a great sense of purpose, was from Tunica, and we had stopped to visit his family while enroute to Orlando, Florida, from Great Lakes, Illinois. We had just graduated from the Navy's Basic Electrical and Electronics School in Great Lakes and were on our way to Orlando to attend the Navy's Nuclear Power School. Dexter was not at all excited about visiting his hometown. I thought that to be a bit odd, but once there, I fully understood why he struggled to generate any positive emotion related to this short visit home. In the early 1980s, during the time I visited, the town of Tunica had an infamous row of ramshackle homes built in the 1950s positioned along an open sewer ditch. The poverty-stricken residents of the 100 or so dwellings, most without plumbing or electricity, carried their feces, urine, and dirty water in buckets and disposed of them in the open sewer trench that the ramshackle homes lined along. The odor emitting from the sewer ditch was overwhelmingly odiferous. I have no words to describe the odiferous stench of the trench. Additionally, the manner of life I observed in the Sugar Ditch Region, the actual name given to this area, was just as disturbing as the smell of the trench. I was born and raised in impoverished conditions myself, but the conditions I observed in Tunica, Mississippi, were unfathomable. Not in my wildest imagination did I imagine that humans lived in such circumstances anywhere in America. These horrid and inhumane conditions were well concealed just a few yards beyond the downtown buildings in Tunica, and the most ironic part of it all was the name given to the area. This wretched and forsaken little community was referred to as the "Sugar Ditch." Dexter had spent a good portion of his life in the Sugar Ditch district of Tunica. He had joined the Navy to escape these inhumane conditions of social living. His family still resided in Tunica, and that was why we were visiting. Sugar Ditch, Mississippi, gained national attention in the mid-1980s, shortly after our visit, when Reverend Jessie Jackson and a few local politicians brought national attention to the deplorable situation. Today, the shacks are gone, and the open sewer has been replaced with a county-maintained underground sewer system. However, the sewer ditch may not have been the worst of it. In the early 1980s, Tunica, Mississippi, was also infamous for having the worst education system and the worst economy in America. More than half of the county residents were on welfare or some form of government assistance then.

The demographics of Tunica were approximately 70% Black and 30% White. And the majority population was pushed oppressively into the margins of one of the most racist states in the nation. Most of the working Blacks, not far removed from slavery, were sharecroppers picking cotton for less than federal minimum wage. Sugar Ditch was where Tunica sharecroppers resided and lived off government subsidies. Unemployment, poor hygiene, no access to quality health care, and undereducation were synonymous with living in Sugar Ditch in 1984. I have never forgotten Sugar Ditch, Mississippi. I have often mentally revisited the shocking human conditions I observed. I have also wondered on many occasions: How does one find themselves afflicted by such trials as living within a few feet of an open sewer trench filled with human bodily waste and do nothing to impact their life? How does one consign their life to the conditions of a sugar ditch and relatively deprive themselves of a better existence?

Relative deprivation is the way a person perceives their situation compared to another or a group experiencing a similar situation in lifestyle, health, economic condition, social status, or power. Essentially, a person feels deprived to the degree to which they feel have less than, equal to, or more than someone who has more than, equal to, or less than them. A person may feel relatively deprived if they lack the means to sustain the equal lifestyle, health, economic condition, social status, or power of another or others in the group. For instance, one may feel that their house is too small if they live in a neighborhood where everyone else's house is much bigger than theirs. Therefore, they feel relatively deprived of owning a large house because they may believe they have the right to own a large house since everyone in their immediate neighborhood has one. A woman may

PRINCIPLE FOUR: NOW

feel inadequately adorned if her wedding ring includes only a quarter of a carat diamond when her girlfriends have wedding rings that include two carat or bigger diamonds. This refers to the inferiority one feels when one compares oneself to others and realizes that they have less than what they believe themselves to be entitled to compared to others in the group. I refer to this as "the inferiority conundrum created by the perceived deficit in current amenities when current amenities are compared to perceived entitlements." The self-assumed deficit between what one has and what one believes one should have is recognized as normal human responses. How humans respond to this deficit is precisely what separates my friend Dexter from those who remained in substandard living conditions in Tunica, Mississippi, or any other city in America where similar conditions exist. Dexter had a great sense of self-worth and wanted more than what he envisioned being able to acquire if consigned to an inferior life living next to an open sewer ditch. So, he did what I expect most of us would do, at least the ones rightly motivated by relative deprivation. He joined the military and got the hell out of Tunica, Mississippi. He refused to consign himself to a life where his most obvious options were picking cotton at minimum wages and living next to an open trench filled with human filth or trying to survive off government assistance programs in a sugar ditch. Dexter understood that the military would provide him with a greater vantage point in life than Tunica, Mississippi. He understood that life was about timing, awareness, and position, and he recognized that Sugar Ditch was not the best position. Thus, he seized the opportunity to improve his position in life with purpose and vision.

One may ask; "What does Tunica, Mississippi, Sugar Ditch, and Dexter Clancy have to do with becoming an exceptional leader?" That is a great question! The answer is, "They have plenty to do with exceptional leadership." Sugar Ditch, Mississippi, existed because there were humans willing to consign themselves to such inferior circumstances and do nothing to impact their lives. One exists in a sugar ditch anytime they feel no sense of being entitled to better human conditions to the point that they view any offered situation as acceptable, even when what is offered is within a few feet of an open sewer trench. *No man, by nature, is inferior to another. Inferiority is a self-assumed existence. In the grand scheme of things, there are no permanent assignments of status. One can always increase their position in life, irrespective of current circumstance; therefore, one consigns to inferiority if they do nothing on their own behalf to impact their condition.* In terms of leadership, *in the grand scheme of leadership, no leader, by nature, is a poor leader. The lower levels of leadership are self-assumed positions of leadership. A leader can always become a better leader, irrespective of current circumstances; therefore, one consigns to poor leadership if they do nothing on their own behalf or on behalf of their team or organization to impact current conditions.* My friend Dexter would eventually become a commissioned officer in the United States Armed Forces. He currently holds the position of district superintendent of the California public school system. Dexter may never have had such opportunities if he had not first bettered his position. Because he bettered his position by getting the hell out of Tunica, Mississippi, he was able to later take advantage of the timing of opportunities that came his way. People lived in Sugar Ditch in Tunica, Mississippi, because of their willingness to accept those horrible conditions. Like Dexter, every person in Tunica and everywhere else in this country has the option to move beyond current conditions to better their position. As a leader, success

PRINCIPLE FOUR: NOW

is often determined by your position and awareness. We have no control over time. If you find yourself in a leadership dead spot or organizational sugar ditch, you need to take immediate action to change your current circumstances.

Being in the NOW does not imply that leadership is stagnant. In fact, it implies the opposite. The exceptional leader takes actions to move himself or herself and his or her organization forward at all times, incessantly. An exceptional leader ensures that his or her actions are never restricted. An exceptional leader never allows circumstances such as those described above in Tunica, Mississippi, to have the final word on the level of success achieved. The exceptional leader is always in the NOW, constantly navigating and maneuvering in an attempt to be in the right place, at the right time, and fully aware of every opportunity. What can the exceptional leader do to ensure that he or she is in the NOW and TAPPED IN? They must be self-motivated to develop professionally with intensity and fervently increase knowledge with a global perspective.

A Leadership Performance Perspective: *Intensity and knowledge are about coming to a particular revelation about yourself and the greatness you are pursuing. Knowledge should always reveal something that advances your leadership abilities—causing you to grow personally and professionally. Revelation is about revealing what is already inside you. Revelation is an internal proposition in which every day you live, work, and play, you should be engaged in something that allows you to revel in it. Do you revel in your leadership? Do you revel in your greatness? Do you revel in your vision, passion, and purpose? If you are reveling in what has been revealed, then you are operating in the NOW. Navigate, organize, and view your* *life in a manner that causes you to be TAPPED IN at all times. When you are TAPPED IN, the stars become the destination, and every leader should be striving to become a star, if for no other reason than the fact that others are following. You want to make sure you are taking them somewhere they want to go so that they can revel in their greatness. Greatness Is What Greatness Does. You revel in knowing what you are destined to become. Your career has been revealed to you; you simply must live it. You can live it because you operate in the NOW and always remain TAPPED IN. So, the day you get your big opportunity to lead, revel in your new leadership role because the role has already been revealed to you. What has been revealed to you? Revel in it!*

A Leadership Development Perspective: *While I fully understand that one can meet some degree of opposition and resistance to their upward movements in the workplace, an employee's response to the theory of relative deprivation determines the degree of pressure they apply to any such resistance. When one feels marginalized by having limited opportunities for promotion and does nothing to increase the chances for promotion, such as going back to college and getting a degree or an additional degree, they are electing to operate in a sugar ditch of self-stultification. The American workforce, in this atmosphere of globalization, is extremely competitive. A person may find that their upward movement is opposed, but each person must understand that it is always possible to better one's chances for upward mobility in any organization. How a leader or emerging leader approaches adversity in the workplace can be critical to professional and leadership development. Circumstances of adversity in the workplace, just like the wretched conditions of the Sugar Ditch region of Tunica, Mississippi, require one to concentrate resources and focus greatly on the opportunity at hand. If one is not operating* *in favorable conditions in the workplace, they must be proactive in partnering with the human resources function of the organization and learn what options are available that will better their chances for a promotion or whatever they seek. Vision, being aware of opportunities, and determination to be in the right place at the right time define the future in the workplace just as they determine the outlines of life. I recall a conversation with a colleague in which she stated: "I remember being married with four children and working on my second degree. I was working on obtaining my master's degree so I could better my opportunities in the workplace. I had a husband who did not support my commitment to better my position. One evening, I was scheduled to take a final exam at the University of California, Davis (UC Davis). My husband refused to care for the kids so that I could go take the exam that would allow me to qualify for my degree. Instead of consigning myself to a position inferior to my full potential, I loaded my four children, ranging from ages 2 to 7, in my minivan and drove to UC Davis to take my exam. Before leaving home, I fed my children, gave them their baths, and dressed them in their pajamas. I also loaded toys, snacks, and other things that would keep them comfortable and safe. I gave my 7-year-old daughter strict instructions on how to care for and watch her sibling, and I arrived at 7:00 PM to take my exam. Yes, I was in a tough situation but not an impossible situation. I admit that leaving my 7-year-old daughter in charge of her three younger siblings for an hour so I could take the exam was a questionable decision. But I was determined to better my condition, so I could better provide for my children." Being an exceptional leader requires making tough decisions that are subject to the scrutiny and opinion of others. My colleague was the leader of her family. She led with intensity, and she was determined to be in the NOW. She was committed to being TAPPED IN. She met much resistance in her own home as she attempted to rise above her current circumstances. But she did not consign to a position of inferiority or defeat. She found ways to overcome her situation. That is what a great leader does, and that is precisely the attitude one must bring into the workplace if one expects to be highly successful at work and in life. When you are willing to navigate with an organizational focus toward a world-class perspective, the universe is prepared to reward you.*

As soon as you are put in a position of leadership and you start to experience a degree of success, fascinating and luxurious opportunities will open before you, and these things are yours by right of your accomplishments. Leadership allows you to get into a place of testing where your own welfare would be the right and proper things to consider. But great leaders are not just interested in their own well-being. Great leaders are intent on caring for the welfare of every individual in the organization, not just what is right for the leader. Whenever "right for self" is made the guidance in leadership, it will blunt out deep leadership insight. The great enemy of leadership in an organization is not the never-ending drive for success but the good which is not good enough. Good enough is always the enemy of best. Many leaders do not reach their best because they prefer to choose what is right for themselves instead of relying on what is best for the organization. Great leaders learn to walk according to the standard that has its eye on what is best and not simply what is right. Good enough should never be considered, for good enough is not best. Good, irrespective of how good, is an inferior position to best, and best goes unrealized. Best can only be realized when leaders operate in the NOW, moving in the right direction with the proper perspective, and are TAPPED IN, at the right place, at the correct time, and fully aware of all opportunities.

A Leadership Development Perspective: *Women can often develop a rescue fantasy, a permanent condition of inferiority. This condition of inferiority can spill into the workplace, manifested in women in leadership who feel they are not as good as their male counterparts. As a result, far too many women have consigned to inferior conditions, believing that they are not as capable as men or that the height of their upward mobility in the workplace and as leaders depends on the quality of the men they can partner with throughout their careers. Similarly, some men can also, especially those who lack immediate economic means, can develop perpetual conditions of inferiority. Men in the workplace compare themselves far too often in an unhealthy manner to other male coworkers. Then relative deprivation rules their lives. An addiction to the unhealthy consumption of good enough makes one inferior because one must consent to the notion that one does not have the capacity or means to help oneself move beyond current positions. In such a despondent disposition, one just waits for the man flying through the air wearing a pantyhose. Superman is not coming to develop you into a great leader! Human resources has a responsibility to ensure that everyone feels entitled to be the best leader possible and strive for more than just what they have a right to. But leaders must be willing to partner with HR in a collaborative effort, not in the spirit of being rescued or false identity but in the spirit of working toward what is best for everyone in the organization.*

Leadership Greatness in Practice: When in positions of leadership, we must fight the temptation to choose what is right and easily within our grasp but rather collaborate with all stakeholders in the organization to choose what is best for all. Timing, awareness, and position become everything. Great leaders do not sit around and wait for someone to rescue them. They do not compare themselves falsely with their coworkers or counterparts. Great leaders who seek what is best never play themselves as the victim of their own self-interest. Self-interest is influenced by low expectations, and good becomes good enough. Too many Americans are willing to live in mediocrity rather than act with an extreme purpose to impact the world in a more positive manner and move mankind closer to our best possible. The depth of life is defined by just how well we understand that our success in leadership, as in life, is subjugated by our timing, awareness, and position. Are we living in the NOW? Are we TAPPED IN or tapped out?

I grew up in the small southern community of Bakewell, Tennessee, approximately 30 minutes north of Chattanooga. Our house was a small and modest three-bedroom one bath house in a neighborhood of small and modest three-bedroom one bath houses. Some homes had running water, and some did not. Everyone was impoverished, and we all were in the margins of existence. We were miles away from Tunica, Mississippi. There was no open sewer ditch in the neighborhood; nonetheless, we lived in a sugar ditch in the community of East Bakewell, Tennessee. We lived in a sugar ditch because no one had much of anything and did not have a healthy sense of entitlement to anything better. We were either too satisfied with nothing or too afraid to impact our impoverished conditions. We were dependent on others who looked upon us in amused contempt for our well-being. There were a few outliers in the community who were better positioned, took advantage of opportunities when the timing was right, and took full responsibility for bettering their social conditions, but most just waited around for the meager offerings from a hostile Southern environment ruled by supremacy that worked endlessly to deprive

PRINCIPLE FOUR: NOW

us of any sense of entitlement. I guess many just didn't believe better was possible and accepted what was offered and refused to demand better. That's a severe sugar ditch to have to crawl out from and carve out a successful life. The sugar ditch provides reference to the actions we take, the choices we make, and our timing and relative proximity to opportunity. Greatness oftentimes has roots in meager beginnings. Very few things in life are as motivating as poverty. Greatness is not defined by where you started but by where you find yourself at life's end. *Greatness Is What Greatness Does.*

My mother, a woman of greatness, demanded the best from her four sons. My mother, the sole reason I have existed outside of the sugar ditch of my circumstances, despite the impoverished social conditions we lived in when I was a child, preached high expectations and striving incessantly to be the absolute best. Every leader must have similar expectations. High expectations produce high levels of performance. My mother was an example and a witness to what one must do when life knocks you down. She did not fall apart when her husband ran out on her. She got busy bettering herself so that she could afford to keep the modest three-bedroom one bath house that she still lived in until the day she passed away. She raised four boys, put one through college, paid off her mortgage, and drove a brand-new car every five or so years. She retired after the age of 65. She was not rich, but she was financially comfortable. This may not seem to be much of an accomplishment to some, but one must first understand the interior landscape of the inferior position from which my mother was forced to carve out five lives and to do such without a high school diploma and without a second income from a husband in a Southern American environment that was very oppressive to women of color. My mother never yielded in her determination to raise four boys to be hardworking gentlemen, gifted with the capacity and ability to positively impact the social conditions of our existence. My mother reminded me and my brothers that no one owed us anything. She told us there were no guarantees in this life and that the world would become what we created. She vehemently preached that a person may find themselves in a ditch through no fault of theirs, but to remain in the ditch would solely be their choice. She drilled into our minds that every man has the ability to alter his conditions. This is worth repeating: Amelia Victoria Jones taught me that *"No man or woman, by nature, is inferior to another. Inferiority is a self-assumed existence. In the grand scheme of things, there are no permanent assignments of status. One can always increase one's position in life, irrespective of current circumstance; therefore, one consigns to inferiority if one does nothing on their own behalf to impact the conditions of life."* Amelia Victoria Jones is the smartest and most courageous woman I have known. My mother possessed every great trait that personifies great leadership. She was what greatness does. She made everyone around her better while driving herself to be better. As a family, we had survived the sugar ditch created by my father's early departure from our family. We were all TAPPED IN. My mother struggled to ensure we had the proper position in life, and she told my brothers and I that we had to stay keenly aware of opportunities and be ready when the time came so we could take advantage of every situated life presented. My mother was not home every night to read to us. My brothers and I did not sit down for home-cooked meals every day. My mother was not available to transport us to basketball, football, or baseball practice. But she was in our minds informing us that we were entitled to a better life. She was there to remind us that we would get from life only what we demanded from life. I would eventually become a nuclear engineer in the United States Navy, obtain several college degrees, rise up the ranks in corporate America, work as a senior administrator in public education, become an author and a publisher, serve on the boards of several community-based organizations, create and operate my own non-profit organizations, start and operate my own leadership and organizational development consulting firm, and raise a beautiful family in a very large home in a neighborhood of very large homes. And I am from a sugar ditch! *Greatness Is What Greatness Does.*

I thought of my plight in life and the lessons from my mother concerning timing, awareness, and position one day a few years back while attending my oldest daughter's soccer practice. I thought and listened as a group of soccer moms discussed their situations at home. The moms were unaware that I had taken interest in their conversation. All but one was very comfortable with their inferior conditions of domesticated servitude, dependent on their husbands. One stay-at-home soccer mom even confided to the group that she did not know what she would do if she had to live without her husband. Her husband provided all the financial support and all medical and dental benefits for the family. I wondered what my life would have been like had my own mom been in such a fragile and vulnerable position in life. Only one soccer mom was the bread winner in her household. She also happens to be my neighbor. Lauren assumes no position under a man. She is in total control of the circumstances that influence the conditions of her life. Lauren does not believe any man is superior to her. She acts with an extreme purpose to have a positive impact on her world and self-decides the quality of social living she and her family experiences. She has no rescue fantasy, and she is not waiting for Superman. Lauren's life mirrors the impoverished conditions that I grew up in. Lauren's mother, like my mother, taught Lauren to be TAPPED IN. Lauren's first husband left her with two very young daughters to raise on her own. She did not crumble under the weight of poverty. Instead, she went back to college and matriculated a course of study in health science. Her two daughters are now college graduates themselves. Lauren owns four separate real estate properties, drives an S-Class Mercedes Benz, and is a senior executive for one of the nation's largest health maintenance organizations. While Lauren loves her current husband dearly, he fully understands that his departure from the family will have no social or economic impact on her life. Lauren is TAPPED IN. In comparison, the other soccer moms are living in a sugar ditch. They may be well educated. They may be living in upscale suburbia. They may not have the stench of the Tunica trench. They may have running water and electricity. They may even have Corinthian columns. But they are not in control of the circumstances that influence the conditions of their lives. The quality of their existence depends primarily on their husbands' ability and desire to continue providing for them. Their lives do not have a sewer ditch running through it, but, otherwise, they are no better off than the impoverished citizens of Tunica, Mississippi. They have settled for the good that their husbands can provide. They have never, and will probably never, experience the best that they can produce with their own actions, motivations, and intellects. The soccer moms were tapped out. They were not positioned to take advantage of opportunities, and their sugar ditch mentality robs them of the ability to recognize when life presents something to them. The soccer moms on my daughter's soccer team were trapped. They had learned how to justify their existence in close proximity to divorced women and maladjusted children. Many people allow themselves to be trapped in mental conditions of mediocrity. People do it to themselves by consigning to lives of dependency and tapping out. We need only to track the daily decisions that confront us to gauge the trajectory of our lives. We are not victims of circumstance. What we do matters in life. We cannot blame the past for an unhappy life today. You may wonder why a book on leadership has such a focus on personal life. Leadership begins at home. Who we are matters. How we were raised matters. Who our parents are matters. Where we hang out matters. All these things matter because they dictate more than any other parts of our lives who exactly we are in the workplace and define our leadership perspectives, styles, and approaches.

Survival, whether in a sugar ditch in Tunica, Mississippi, or in the board room of a Fortune 500 company, always goes to the fittest and the best prepared, not those hanging out in a sugar ditch, bathed in inferiority, and waiting for Superman. All great leaders understand the vital importance of being in the NOW and remaining TAPPED IN always. While Americans have a strong history of great leadership, to continue our greatness, we must fervently engage life as Dexter Clancy and Lauren have and espouse to strength, knowledge, preparation, and wisdom. We are not raising our children in the same manner that my mother raised her four boys. America became the greatest nation on earth because men and women came to this country with a dream and a plan. Those dreams continue to flow today in all our lives. Our forefathers and foremothers built this country from the ground up with their own sweat and tears. They changed their positions by coming to America. They remained vigilant and seized opportunities every chance they had. Their timing was perfect. Our forefathers and foremothers did not sit around all day watching television shows like *Real Housewives of Atlanta* and *Jersey Shores*. They worked hard every day instead of sitting around taking the path of least resistance and assuming positions of inferiority, trapped in fear of death. Our forefathers and foremothers did not hang out on the corner every day in an idle state of dependency. They moved daily without hesitation or inhibition. They were girded with determination and vision, and they were self-sufficient. Dependency is the first stage of a life in a sugar ditch smelling someone else's filth. That is not what greatness does. Greatness shows up every day to work hard. Greatness is self-determined and committed to success. Greatness has high expectations and drives everyone around to reach for their best.

Refusing to act on one's own behalf as a leader to impact one's professional condition prevents a person from gaining access to levels of greatness. The table of this great nation has been prepared by great Americans who assumed strong positions of superiority and acted with extreme entitlement. And upon the table, these great Americans placed opportunity, justice, education, employment, and a voice in American politics and world governance. Opportunity may not be in abundance in every American workplace, justice may be handed down unevenly in our individual professional endeavors, and education for our children may not be the best, but these are exactly the same conditions that Dexter Clancy has faced. Dexter is a Ph.D. from the Sugar Ditch Region of Tunica, Mississippi. Because of Dexter's accomplishments, no American can offer any excuses for doing anything short of their absolute best. Another good friend of mine, Tony Magee, author of the best-selling

PRINCIPLE FOUR: NOW

book *Can't Shove a Great Life Into a Small Dream*, was born and raised in the Watts community of Los Angeles, California, to a single mother. Tony emerged from one of the most violent and poverty-stricken communities of America to become the first African American to earn a master's degree in materials science and engineering from Lehigh University. He also earned an MBA from Pepperdine University. Tony works as an engineer for NASA, coaches corporate America, and influences the world with power and influence as a motivational speaker. The table was prepared for Tony, but he did not just sit at the table and consume whatever others provided for him. Tony planted his own seeds to the successful life he envisioned for himself. He fertilized, grew, and harvested his dreams. Tony did not sit around and watched Jerry Springer all day. Yes, he was from Compton, California, and had to traverse social conditions designed to shatter his dreams. He grew up in the Watts neighborhood, a crime- and gang-infested ghetto in Southern California—another Sugar Ditch like Tunica, Mississippi. Instead of living next to a raw human sewer trench, Tony had to deal with shotguns being pointed at his head and other kids laughing at him because he had to eat brown bananas. Tony did as Dexter did; he got the hell out of his sugar ditch and never looked back. And look at Tony's life now and consider his travels. The lives of Dexter, Lauren, and Tony are phenomenal, especially when you think of the soccer moms living their lives of leisure, privileged since birth, and completely dependent on the existence of a man. Tony, Lauren, and Dexter are examples and witnesses to the fact that no leader, by nature, is inferior to another's leadership. In the grand scheme of things, there are no permanent assignments of social status. One can always increase his or her leadership capacity, irrespective of current circumstance; therefore, one consigns to poor leadership if one does nothing on their own behalf to impact the conditions of their leadership and the success of their organization.

What would the workplace world look like if there were more great leaders like Tony MaGee, Lauren Miller, and Dexter Clancy striving for their best and not just good or good enough? Dexter, Lauren, and Tony are great leaders because they have chosen greatness, operate in the NOW, and remain TAPPED IN. They have acted on their own behalf to impact their personal and leadership greatness. Their greatness has been revealed to them, and like them, you must revel in your greatness as well. There is no separation between personal greatness and leadership greatness. Get in the NOW and become great! *Greatness Is What Greatness Does.*

PRINCIPLE FIVE

Complete

Complete: The Exceptional Leader is complete. He or she is Cubic—of equal measure in the length, width, and height of their leadership.

> *"In a Misery of this Sort, admitting some few Lenities, and those too but a few, nine Parts in ten of the whole Race of Mankind drudge through Life."*
> —*Edmund Burke,* A Vindication of Natural Society, *1752*

As reiteration of the introduction, I have traversed the landscape of our nation, the land of opportunity, coast to coast and North to South times over; as authors, a publisher, motivators, human capacity engineers and leadership development consultants, an attorney, HR Professional, organizational leadership consultant, a psychologist, scholars and many other things. Our vast and privileged experiences with the American culture have extended to us intimate knowledge and provided us extensive observations of an enormous array of human conditions. This, in part, is why, while facilitating a leadership development workshop not long ago in the beautiful city of Tampa, Florida, I felt that I had chosen a topic too far removed from the hearts and minds of the audience, a group of senior public administrators from around the nation, and so failed to interest them as much as I might have done, otherwise. The theme of my lecture was "Discover who you are" in the sense of understanding personal ability and attaining great success based on natural God-given talent and developed capacity. In a private discussion following the lecture, I discussed the experience with my sponsor and petitioned for her insight. My sponsor, a highly successful and very talented businesswoman, reminded me that people are not interested in self-examination. She said my presentation encouraged the awareness and contemplations of painful realities that the mass of men and women go at great lengths to avoid. She said that my lecture illuminated the regions of the mind that very few have traveled. She reminded me, as Henry David Thoreau suggested approximately two centuries ago, that most people already lead desperate lives and are looking only for simple answers and assurances, even if both are false. She stated that Americans only want to be told that America is the greatest place on earth, life is grand, and the world will only get better. I stated that I was keenly aware that men and women are only interested in being told how to quickly possess, with selfish desires, the meaningless little tokens of life that they believe they want. And, with very few exceptions, Americans are not interested in reliving the convulsions that created the dreary situations currently holding them captive. I added that people do not respond well when I describe things and processes not in or near to their hearts but toward their extremities and superficies. I further responded by stating that I believe most men and women have become so impoverished in life, not so much due to the lack of financial means, but by uncontrolled desire to arbitrarily possess material wealth in mastodonic proportions, irrespective of the necessity of life, coupled with undisciplined and diminished capacity for being satisfied with the abundance they already possess. I believe this is the true challenge to leadership in this country. How do you drive a culture of greatness in the workplace when people come to work so extremely fractured emotionally and psychologically? I believe the self-imposed impoverished conditions of life that I speak of is the very cause for many Americans drudging desperately through life, even though life is grand in the land of opportunity, albeit not equal opportunity for all. So, now I would say something similar to you, my readers. I will resist the urge to refer to people, workplaces, and leadership experiences a thousand miles away but come as close to your heart and home as I can. I will intentionally leave out all the adulation of American life, as flattery tends to grow on trees, and retain all the critique, as I have come to understand that the crux of great leadership is only established with careful examination and guided analysis. While perfection is impossible, I do believe we can have far greater human experiences in our leadership endeavors, but we must first be willing to identify and condemn the cause of what decreases us before we can resolve to inherent and sustained increases. After all, greatness is what greatness does. The challenge we face as great leaders, gifted with enormous talents and the power of volition, is the fact that we are superbly talented at making excuses for ourselves and others, and most would much rather be excused than condemned. Very few are willing to publicly or privately confess innate human consequences that describe each of us in less that favorable terms. As Dr. Cornel West so eloquently and honestly stated, *"We're all cracked vessels…attempting to somehow love our crooked neighbors with the crooked hearts we have."* We're all imperfect souls with fractured spirits and impure intentions trying to live harmoniously on this planet. And that is the leadership crux, the decisive point at which we must redesign leadership if we intend to remain the greatest country.

Let us consider for a moment our justifications for the way we lead in the workplace in American, reasoning the poor compensation and marginal lives of others as long as life is grand in the time and space of our leadership. As the mass of humankind is drudging in the workplace and in their varied organizations, making excuses for themselves, and doing desperate things, we must ask: If it is reasonable to believe that people are becoming with increasing facility better adapted to the new American form of leadership that is void of integrity to common goals and without care for the well-being of others, then are we forfeiting our ability to self-liberate the anecdote of true leadership and tell the honest truth about what leadership has evolved into in America? We are not all equally gifted, educated, or wealthy. America is not a monolithic society. There will never be equality in any category of living. It is the extremes of wealth and poverty that tears at the very fabric and culture of the American workforce and, thus, the workplace. In his first inaugural address as president of the United States, Thomas Jefferson said, "*...Let us restore to social intercourse that harmony and affection without which liberty and even life itself are but dreary things.*" While we should commit to striving daily to better our circumstances, our social intercourse will eternally be void of harmony and affection to some degree because, as a nation, we live at the extremes of wealth and poverty. Let us be slow to consider wealth and poverty only in financial terms. Let's consider conditions of wealth and poverty in intellectual, humanitarian, spiritual, planetary, natural, universal, community, family, loving, sentimental, and, yes, leadership terms as well. We are a polarizing people. Too much separates us, not just financially; more importantly, we are separated spiritually, sexually, intellectually, philosophically, and objectively. These are the reasons there is such a deficit of great leadership in this country. Spiritual, kindheartedness, forbearance, and intellectual impoverishments are far more detrimental to the quality of leadership than the lack of money will ever be, for leadership indifference is the spoiled fruit of emotional and mental poverty. Because of human indifference, we are forced to lead in a workplace that is increasingly intellectually confused and philosophically dysfunctional, and the average employee has very few worthy objectives capable of delivering social harmony and affection in the workplace. This is simply the result of leadership that is disconnected from the well-being of others and void of spiritual astuteness. The truth about who we are individually and what we are collectively truly capable of tends to be staggeringly and destructively unimportant in our American way of leading others. More is better, bigger is the goal, winning is the only option, and uncontrollable desire is king. We are one-dimensional, selfish, and self-centered in our perpetual pre-occupation with wealth accumulation and being the biggest bad ass on the block. The more we get, the more we want. The more we want, the more impoverished we become. The more impoverished we become, the more desperate we are. And it is that very sense of desperation at the extremities of leadership where there exists no form of harmony and affection within our social intercourse or in our workplaces. This is the unwavering condemnation and embarrassing leadership legacies being passed from generation to generation in America. We can and must do better! *Greatness Is What Greatness Does.*

    Great friends of mine have parented two daughters together. Both daughters are college graduates. The oldest daughter is gainfully employed, has a boyfriend, and lives with female roommates. The youngest daughter is unemployed and lives with her boyfriend. My friends currently are indebted to pay two school loans. The oldest daughter is substantially supported by my good friends. They pay the insurance for the car they purchased for her. They pay her cell phone bill, help with her rent, and pay for all her vacations abroad. The youngest daughter is fully supported financially by my good friends. They pay everything from her cell phone bill to gas for the automobile they purchased for her to her apartment rent to her vacations abroad. Of my friends, one works as a police officer and private investigator, and the other works as a public safety dispatcher. They are not wealthy by any stretch of the imagination. In fact, they have lost a home to foreclosure, are severely indebted with various consumer debt, and have very poor credit ratings. Nevertheless, the daughters ask for more, and my friends give them more. The daughters feel so entitled at this point, and even worse, they have been empowered by a reality created by their parents, my great friends. Children do not erect their circumstances; they simply adapt to the adult-defined and cultivated environments to which they are subjugated. As adults and parents, we should avoid establishing any set of conditions that will provide for our children to be able to afford doing nothing with their lives. Rather, the goal should be that our children grow healthily into adulthood handsomely adorned with all the necessities for doing anything they wish to do with their lives. And if we, as the environment creators, do our jobs correctly, our children will champion more than simply leeching and laboring as spoiled brats. Interestingly enough, I offered similar advice to my great friends, as they solicited me for advice on how to bring about the demise of the entitlement culture they have created for their children, to no avail. The youngest will soon be exploring Germany on an all-expense, paid by mommy and daddy, vacation, even though she graduated from college more than a year ago and has refused to find employment. My good friends also recently fully furnished an apartment for their youngest daughter and her boyfriend. In America, we have created this human-made disease called entitlement that cripples our children at birth and stunts their progressive and healthy assimilation into a savory and joyous existence with society and the universe. If you closely observe the environment around you, you will become vividly aware that our children and many adults live as if nature does not exist. Would your child choose enjoying a sunset or a sunrise over driving a BMW? Our children live wanting more, more, more, as if nature is incidental to whom and what we are, and we need to stop blaming kids for being a product of the environment that we adults have created. Now, you are asking, "What does the last passage have to do with leadership?" The children I just described will be 75% of the American workforce by 2030. And how do we lead a workforce rot with Americans with an entitlement disposition?

Not everyone can drive a BMW to work, but every employee can want one. Such arbitrary demand on financial pursuits can cause destitution and a sense of worthlessness, the condition of being without something of extreme value and importance in our lives when the means are not sufficient for satisfying the demand. As for the comparative command with which we encourage our children to make choices in life and the imposition of the same command upon ourselves, it is a very important to differentiate between two mindsets. In one instance, one is satisfied with a certain level of success. One's aim in life results in hitting the intended mark every time. In the other instance, however unsuccessful one's life may be, one constantly elevates the target, though very slightly to make the goal seemingly easy to attain. Each of us should be challenged beyond what is easily in our grasp, as an aim that is too low decreases life, and an aim that is too high results in disenfranchisement with life, resulting in an impoverished condition. As an old Chinese Proverb says, *"Greatness does not approach him who is forever looking down, and all those who are looking high are growing poor."* If we can somehow avoid destitution and worthlessness as self-imposed conditions of inescapable inequality, dominated by a constant upward gaze, as a circumstance of uncontrollable want of material things, then we can prevent desperation and poverty from afflicting generation after generation of leadership, for life will always present the increase for the undisciplined and impoverished to unhealthily aspire to. We must be of a more conscious mind, especially in matters relating to our children, for they are the American workforce of the future.

We are a nation in which 2% of the population controls 50% of the wealth, and 5% controls 75%. The remaining 95% of the population is in constant fear of losing the material life each have so desperately erected and slipping downward into an oppressive existence void of desired material possessions. Men possess most of the wealth in the world, while women attempt suicide at a rate three times that of men, although men are more successful at taking their own lives. Economic means, or the lack thereof, is advertised to be one of the major causes of suicidal ideations for men and women. Has the pursuit of happiness and the American Dream really become so serious of an endeavor to keep up with the Joneses that failure to keep pace graduates the individual to despair and despondence? What if the American way of life, in the end, is really only about chattel possession and personal prosperity? Perhaps the American way is more about having a big bank account and less about moral astuteness. Can it be that Americans are more consumed with attaining financial wealth and personal security than we are focused on the noble human characteristics of honesty, integrity, and trustworthiness? As I lecture nationally and discern spiritually, I see those faces in the crowd that are after so much more out of life. I hear their passionate and desperate pleads. Unfortunately, the things we are begging for more and more of are far too often categorized as meaningless material possessions that only drive us to want more of the same. While I strive, in my writings, lectures, and public discourse, to encourage worthier pursuits of life—kindheartedness, astute character, helping others, loving relationships, spiritual atonement, and great leadership—I have to admit that I believe most in attendance are there simply to gain knowledge to advance their position at the wealth table. History has proven that moral turpitude comes at a price. Can we continue to afford the bill? If so, who's going to pay?

> *"The mass of men leads lives of quiet desperation. What is called resignation is confirmed desperation. From the desperate city you go into the desperate county and have to console yourself with the bravery of minks and muskrats. A stereotyped but unconscious despair is concealed even under what are called the games and amusements of mankind. There is no play in them, for this comes after work. But it is a characteristic of wisdom not to do desperate things."*
> —*Henry David Thoreau,* from Walden

I joined a good friend of mine for happy hour at a restaurant not too long ago. My friend, an extremely successful dentist who owns his dental practice, arrived in a new automobile, a new Jaguar XJL. The vehicle is an impressive luxury automobile accomplishment by every stretch of the imagination. I also own a Jaguar, an XJR model. My vehicle is an older 2016 model. As my friend and I engaged initially in conversation dominated by this "super bad" new Jaguar he just drove up in, it became strikingly clear to me that the root cause of poor leadership, at home and at work, was wanting to the point of deficit. Impoverishment is not defined by one's ability to run out and immediately purchase a Jaguar or some other meaningless material chattel but by the magnitude to which one's current material chattel no longer is capable of producing satisfaction once a want has developed. Poverty exists when there is a spiritual, financial, social, ethical, or human deficit in life conditions in relationship to the inherent circumstances giving cause to one's dissatisfaction with their current situation or relative to the degree to which one has self-control in managing a particular want in life. If my friend's new Jaguar created an uncontrolled desire in my soul to the extent that my current 2017 Jaguar XJR no longer satisfied me, then I am instantly impoverished to the degree that I am deficit in controlling my envy from becoming an insatiable meaningless want. If there is a want, there is a potential deficit. If there is a deficit, there is poverty. This applies to leadership as well. Poverty in leadership will exist to the degree that there is a deficit in your leadership conditions and to the level to which your leadership want has become uncontrollable. Want, and, therefore, inequality, in the sense of having less than what another has, is unavoidable. But desperation, the condition of being willing to sacrifice anything for the satisfaction of

PRINCIPLE FIVE: COMPLETE

selfish desires in such a manner that reason, self-discipleship, and even emotional well-being is so fractured as to eventually impede life itself, is not. Great leadership must be more about the well-being of others and the organization and less about the material wants of the leader. The cure for such an impediment, a malady of impoverishment, is not money but a healthy and reasonable degree of desire for the forward progression of life without the unnecessary disdain for the life currently being lived. When life is inhibited by learned desires of the flesh, there exists a disconnection from nature and the universe that destroys the soul of the leader. When we allow ourselves to be completely conjoined with the natural life and greater human pursuits with increasing facility in such a manner to extrapolate every ounce of joy and happiness availed in the universe, irrespective of social status and silly material wants, then we allow ourselves the opportunity to live life richly and abundantly—a type of richness and joy that no amount of money or any type of automobile can provide. And what we feel is instant. What we experience is the innate greatness in leading others to their greatness.

Humankind, since the beginning of time, has never failed to portray the race as being willing to sacrifice everything in a justifiable fashion to get whatever we believe we want. To want for anything is to be incomplete in some dimension. From one end of life to the other, every person strives to succeed at feeling whole or complete. Everyone desires to satisfy their wants by any means necessary. But we are never satisfied! Drunken euphoria may not be the objective, but for the mass of humankind, the insatiable desires of the heart and mind produce the boisterous and continual chorus, "I want MORE, MORE, MORE!!" We may not quite know exactly what will make our life complete, but the very distinct feeling of incompleteness is undeniable, often times oppressive, and never fully satiated. What makes us feel so incomplete and never satisfied? Do humans perceive happiness to be of an infinite measure and therefore believe that the purpose of life is to become a glutton for pleasure and joy? Or is joy the most addictive drug known to humankind that has us chasing that first high for our entire lives? Perhaps the real issue of incompleteness is that humankind has no human concept for what truly the measures of a complete life are. What exactly makes a man or woman whole? What makes leadership complete?

Economy, the accumulation and management of financial wealth not life, love, and happiness, is the primary objective of human striving and measuring in relation to a complete life. Everyone has an overwhelming and overreaching desire to possess strong economic means. Leaders, while our wants are insatiable, intend daily for their organizations to grow in revenue and profit and for the organizations' financial means to exceed their material desires. Every leader wants to lead a big company. After all, bigger is better, isn't it? Economic status is one of the more common manners in which men and women measure the degree to which they have succeeded in life and at work. Was Steve Jobs really more successful than the executive director of the local community-based nonprofit that feeds the homeless? How do we measure greatness in this country? Even a woman who has nothing to call her own expects the man she settles with to have the means of supplying her every want. And every man expects to have a specific level of success to attract the woman he believes will satisfy his needs as a man. In either case, finances become a determinate of success. While success has been given a variety of definitions over the years,

PRINCIPLE FIVE: COMPLETE

and there is no one manner of measuring the degree to which we succeed, the incessant efforts engaged toward securing some arbitrary economic destination dominates our very existence and our leadership endeavors. The innate problem associated with any enterprise created and deployed for the sole purpose of monetary gains projects the entire race downward. Labor is a curse handed down by God to punish man for his disobedience. Man is cursed to have to labor for a living. For that reason, to do anything merely to earn money, without exception, increases want and, therefore, poverty. We are rich in direct proportion to how much we can live without. The more you want, the poorer you are. The poorer you are, the more incomplete you become. If all you do is work, work, work for more, more, more, you truly cheat yourself and others of the true benefits of your natural talents and your ultimate capacity to impact humankind more admirably. So as great leaders, what are we really pushing our employees to accomplish that is meaningful? Laboring strictly for money is a one-dimensional proposition. To be great at only one thing and prostitute your popularity and great leadership skills for only economic gains is to go down precipitously. You are paid for being something less than human when you pimp your talents to the highest bidder. The complete life, where a person is whole in their existence, is multi-dimensional; it is a life worth living; it is a life where you attend to your personal gains, care for the well-being of others, and reach up to God in equal measure. You are cubic in your existence. You are a cubic leader. You are whole with capacity. You no longer want because there exist no deficits in your human conditions when you are whole and complete. You cease making money and start building greater cubic capacity in yourself and others. Making money becomes incidental to you living in completeness. In my opinion, God made the light of the day for much worthier toil than simply making money. And it is the much worthier pursuits that increase the length, width, and height of life, which are the true cubic measures of a complete life of leadership.

Personal Perspective on Leadership: *Be the amazing person God created you to be. Be amazingly wonderful because you are. Being the amazing person God created you to be is determined by the instrument you use to measure yourself. There are three measurements of your complete life; length, width, and height; and the instrument you select to measure your life determines just how great you are. Life is not about comparing yourself to me or anyone else. Not everyone can play at the highest level in the NFL. Not everyone can lead a Fortune 500 company. Not everyone can be a championship NASCAR driver. But everyone can be a complete leader of equal measure in length, width, and height—cubic in their leadership. You are being amazingly wonderful when you are complete, and amazingly wonderful is how God created all of us. You just have to use the correct instrument to measure your leadership greatness. Remember, your greatness is your greatness. Be the leader God created you to be.*

The length, width, and height of life concept lends itself as a vehicle for expressing leadership success as a measurable unit, not just a human condition of uncontrollable and undisciplined selfish desire, and everyone wants to be successful and complete. Whatever the perception is of success, one fact is supreme: the percentage of time actually involved in enjoying successes in life wanes tremendously to the amount of time drudging desperately to attain such successes. Drudgery is not living, irrespective of what it produces. Drudgery is working some unfulfilling job where the only goal is to make money. If a woman labors drudgingly much of her day just to put a meager amount of food on the table, provide modest shelter, and provide a movie once a month as entertainment for herself and her children, to what measure can she reference a degree of enjoyment in her life? Desire will become her addiction, and she will surely perish. If a man's economy requires that he is drudgingly absent from his household but one weekend a month, how complete of a life does he and his family have, even though the handsome compensation for his out-of-town job may have him and his family comfortably situated in middle-class suburbia? Desire will also be his drug, and his life will be imperiled onto the spike of desperation. I believe leaders, men and women, focus far too much attention on economy to the detriment of living a complete and enjoyable life in leadership. Leadership has become more about economic, social, and professional strife, and less about the genuine enjoyment of life and care for others.

Let's consider a biblical metaphor of the human measures of a complete life in reference to what great leadership really looks like. In the Holy Bible, in the book of Revelation, Chapter 21, John describes a vision in which he refers to as the New Jerusalem descending from Heaven. In part, John describes the New Jerusalem as being 12,000 stadia (7,200,000 feet) in length and said that the measurements of the walls of the new city were equal in length, width, and height. The New Jerusalem was cubic, 7,200,000 feet in all three dimensions. There is no intention to offer a layperson's interpretation of religious text, as I am not suggesting that anyone consider me to be a Master of Theology. But the insight into my own life and how I receive John's vision lead me to believe that John was describing not a place we are to strive to ascend to at life's end, but a human condition we are challenged to develop within our lifetime in this realm. I believe John was describing what each person is to become.

Each person, in their lifetime, is to become metaphorically a New Jerusalem and equal in splendor. The New Jerusalem was complete because it was cubic, equal in its three dimensions: length, width, and height. According to John, in the book of Revelation, the new city is protected by walls made of jasper and is 144,000 cubits thick. That measure is approximately 336 feet, or the length of a football field, thick. I assert that humans are to become cubic, equal in our three dimensions, and we are to be as protective of our cube as a wall of jasper thick as the length of a football field suffices.

Dr. Marin Luther King, Jr., in a sermon in which he also referenced John's vision in Revelation, described the "Dimensions of Life" as follows: Length is the measure of a reasonable degree of healthy selfishness applied toward your own personal achievements in life, width is the measure of your other-people centeredness given to the care and well-being of others and their achievements in life, and height is the measure of your ecumenical reach up to God as ruler of your life. Most of us give great measure to only one dimension of life, and the other two measures are either completely ignored or insignificantly engaged. We are addicted to desire and encapsulated in a one-dimensional abyss. This is the very reason a billionaire can be living such a downward and miserable life. No amount of money makes a person complete, and the lack of money does not limit a person from being whole. A person may have a life of great length, as they may have significant financial means, but their spirit can be dead, and so they do nothing for others. Because that person's life is one-dimensional and not complete, their life is full of dreary things, and there is no social harmony to be had. A person may have a life of wondrous width, as they give in very large proportion for the care and well-being of others but forsake themselves spiritually and humanly. This person is also incomplete. And there are others who may believe in giving all their time to living spiritually and having great height of life while doing nothing for anyone, not even themselves. In all such cases, we are not living a complete life. We feel empty because we have measurable substance in only one dimension. The greatest among us achieves measurable substance in two of the three dimensions, perhaps. But the grand pursuit ought not to be simply for worthless economy. Humans are capable of far greater triumphs than laboring for money just to satisfy uncontrollable wants. Great leaders understand that they must be cubic, of equal measure in length, width, and height. The grand pursuit of great leadership is completeness, to be as cubic as the New Jerusalem, equally measuring 7,200,000 feet at length, width, and height. Everyone who desires to be a great leader, if they truly desire completeness in their leadership, must tend to the needs and well-being of others under their leadership in equal measure to their care for themselves and their healthy selfish desires to be extremely successful. Additionally, great leaders are to reach up to God in equal measure to their leadership achievements. Such lengths, widths, and heights are the measures of a complete cubic leadership and the sure process for achieving excellence.

When a great leader has accomplished some great feat, they want to be recognized in some way. That recognition becomes a little measure of success on some level. Whether the will to achieve and excel is of a natural sense or of a personal motivation, everyone tends to want more out of this human existence. Everyone is in grand pursuit, and success, happiness, love, and emotional wealth are measured in various ways as we travel down Gulliver's path. However success is measured, I believe the reason we attempt to measure our successes and triumphs in life is because we are ultimately striving to live that complete life, or at least that more complete life, even though we are unaware of the gravitational force exerted upon our psyche by God's design of this three-dimensional human existence. As a great leader achieves their great lengths in life professionally and personally, an equal measure of achievement should be experienced by others around them due only to their personal connection with the success of the great leader. As great leaders labor in equal measure for their well-being and for the well-being of others in their association, everyone will achieve greatness. To become a great leader is to become cubic. Be of great and equal measure in your leadership length, width, and height. *Greatness Is What Greatness Does.*

"America is the most grandiose experiment the world has seen, but I am afraid, it is not going to be a success."

— Sigmund Freud

PRINCIPLE SIX

Intensity

Intensity: Exceptional Leadership is exceptionally intense. Intensity pushes you to your maximum. It pushes you to be exceptional in everything you do.

> *"Leading people is the most challenging and, therefore, the most gratifying undertaking of all human endeavors."*
> —Jocko Willink

Leadership intensity is the extreme strength, force, energy, or feeling one exerts in a position of leading others that pushes the collective to reach their maximum in performance. Consider being the leader of an average American family of five—a mother, a father, and three children. Raising children and living in reference to the wants and needs, the emotions and perceptions, and the philosophies and attitudes of another adult human, whether that other human is your wife or husband, is an enormous challenge. Maintaining a healthy marriage and getting your children off to an amazing start in life is arguably the most intense of all human endeavors because of the nature of the relationships involved. As the leader of a family, extreme strength, force, energy, love, and affection are required to push each family member to become the best version of themselves. The challenge can be as great in leading those outside of your family unit, such as in the workplace, on a sports team, or in a community-based organization. For the most part, in most cases, everyone within your family unit of five or so wants to be there and have a vested interest in the family's success. In the family setting, one can easily see the connection of the family succeeding tied tightly to their own well-being. In the organizational setting of the workplace, those connections are not so vivid, and not everyone is as vested in your success as much as they are vested in their own success. In either case, at home or at work, why is leading other people the most daunting undertaking of all human endeavors? While we go to work to support our families, we do not go to work to live as a family. At home, the motivation to live in harmony with others is guided by love and affection for those we share a bloodline with. The family life is a life of sacrifice, sacrificing your own desires for the desires of others—your spouse and children. A mother or father is often heard saying, "I would give my last breath for my family." That's intense! At work, there is very little consideration or thought given to sacrificing for a coworker or a cause, much less giving one's life for the company's success. An often heard reframe is, "No job is worth dying for." So how does one become a great leader of a group of individuals who believe the job is not worth dying for? How does one lead a group of individuals toward a common set of goals within a major corporation if there is no love or affection to help motivate and inspire? Paychecks alone are not what pushes individuals to aspire to greatness. Great leaders inspire others toward greatness. We can look at a great family and see that it is led by a great head of the family. As parents, we never stop wanting more and more for our kids. Not only do we want more, but we also want the more to be the best as well. An extreme measure of strength, force, energy, willpower, passion, and commitment is what brings out the best in ourselves and others. As the head(s) of the household, we are never satisfied with today's success. We strive constantly to increase the savings accounts, the kids' education attainments, our personal development, and the overall capacity of the family. The youngest and least capable receive plenty of support, energy, encouragement, and affection from every other member of the family. When one succeeds in the family unit with a job promotion or a college degree or hits a homerun, scores a touchdown, wins a spelling bee championship, gets a good medical check-up, or is elected to president of the local community-based nonprofit, everyone in the family celebrates. Leading a family is intense. Such intensity is the very force that pushes everyone to reach their maximum in life. The workplace needs the same level of intensity, often times more.

The most common organizational chart will list, in descending order, the CEO or president, senior management, middle management, supervisors, and then workers in a pyramidal diagram of sort. This form of organization requires extreme measures of strength, force, energy, and feelings to push everyone in the organization to be their best. Very few organizations have ever done it well, and the larger the organization is, then the more challenging the pursuit of greatness or the high-performance endeavor becomes. In large pyramidal organizations, intensity in strength, force, energy, feelings, passion, love, and affection is either delegated down or processed out. Unfortunately, in the typical top-down hierarchal organization, the leadership intensity levels become minimal due to the nature of how responsibilities are delegated, and ownership of processes are avoided. Delegating tasks to subordinate management personnel should not result in the leader detaching himself or herself from the process. Leadership delegation should not lead to leadership detachment, but in far too many instances in top-down hierarchal organizations, that's precisely what happens. For example, if you are the CEO of Walmart, a company I previously worked for, you have the opportunity to take no ownership for what happens in any of the approximately 10,000 stores that Walmart operates worldwide if you elect to do so. There are layers after layers between you and the 100,000 plus associates who gather the shopping carts in the 10,000 parking lots or the 1,000,000 plus associates who stock the shelves or unload the trucks at the 10,000 stores. In fact, as the CEO of Walmart, you will never visit the overwhelming majority of Walmart stores. When there is a rare visit, the CEO does not engage in the stocking process or the truck unloading process. There is no human possibility that allows the CEO to visit all 10,000 stores and observe every single process that occurs in a Walmart store. If the CEO made a commitment to visit three stores a day, and that would be extremely aggressive considering all of the other responsibilities of leading the largest company in the world with more than two million employees, it would take him approximately 3,333 days or 10 years to visit all of the stores. As a result, Walmart's CEO very seldom visits any stores. Instead, he delegates the tasks of visiting stores to his subordinate management staff and essentially detaches himself from the process. Not only is visiting stores delegated down, so are strength, force, energy, and feelings. In an organization as large as Walmart, every store has to operate as its own individual company—a company within a company. There is no amount of human intensity possible that can penetrate the enormous organizational layers required to operate a company of two million employees. As a part of Walmart Stores management, I personally never saw anyone from Walmart's senior management. In the approximately 5 years I spent with the company, my stores were visited by the market manager every few months and the regional manager twice a year but never by the business unit manager or anyone else above that level in the company. The leaders in Bentonville took no ownership of what I was doing as local management, and I felt no obligation to concern myself with the goals and mission of leaders who I knew I would never have the opportunity to personally engage. Senior management was disconnected and detached from me and the work I did, and I was disengaged from the goals and mission of the company. There were absolutely no actions of love or affection to motivate or inspire greatness in me coming from Bentonville, and I had absolutely no feelings of love or affection toward anyone in a position of senior leadership within the company. I was totally disconnected from Bentonville, and Bentonville avoided taking ownership of any process I was managing. I felt no intense levels of strength, force, energy, or feelings emitting from Arkansas. How does one serve as the CEO of a company that has two million employees and do it with such intensity that they are completely connected with what motivates and inspires greatness in every employee? Is that even possible? To the degree that such intensity is possible, that is the exact degree to which a company approaches greatness, for greatness is what greatness does. Being the largest company does not make the company the greatest company. Greatness is being as connected to the needs of the porters who clean the restrooms as much as you are connected to the desires of the stakeholders in the boardroom. Greatness is caring about the socioeconomic conditions of everyone employed as much as you care about the profits and losses of the company. Greatness is loving your employees as much as you love your family members, and a leader cannot delegate the tasks of developing love and affection toward employees to another subordinate manager. You cannot effectively lead, motivate, and/or inspire an individual or a group of individuals to greatness if you don't love them enough to show them some affection. And you can't show anyone affection if you never show up in person. That statement holds true in the workplace as well as it does at home with family. Leadership in strength, force, knowledge, energy, passion, commitment, love, and affection must be intense if leadership is to produce greatness. Great leadership is a "hands on every critical process" proposition, and it's extremely intense!

Extreme leadership intensity is taking ownership for the success of every employee and every process in your company. Extreme leadership intensity is visiting every location within the company and building relationships of love and affection that motivates and inspires everyone to levels of greatness. Extreme leadership intensity is shaking the hands of the associates who push shopping carts in the cold, snow, and rain as often as you shake hands in the boardroom. Extreme leadership intensity is taking the responsibility to remain connected even when the size of the organization requires you to delegate leadership tasks. Extreme leadership intensity is fully understanding that leadership is not a position of privilege but an innate level of responsibility. Whether you are the chief of police of a small police department of 100 or less law enforcement officers or that of 40,000 officers, your level of extreme leadership intensity determines the level of greatness both you and your organization will achieve. Leading 40,000 officers is much more intense than leading 100 officers, but one must understand that great intensity is required to be a great chief of police in either department. Remember, you cannot delegate the tasks of love and affection toward your subordinate personnel. That is an extreme leadership responsibility of the highest order. When you visit your local Walmart store or the local city clerk's office or call your local utility company's customer service division, you instantly observe whether leadership is fully engaged and capable. You are immediately aware of whether the CEO of Walmart, the city's mayor, or the utility company's general manager has delegated down the tasks of engaging the human dynamics that determine the greatness of an organization.

Leadership Greatness in Practice: *Being the president of a large community-based national organization is a position of intense leadership. Leading a community-based organization of volunteers with distinguished accomplishments, such as superior court judges, emergency room surgeons, CEOs, business owners, chiefs of police, Ph.Ds., MDs, and JDs, is an intense proposition of keeping men and women of distinction motivated, inspired, and fully engaged in the mission of the national office and the local needs of the community we serve in. Leading people in general is an enormous challenge. Leading a group of volunteers who represent the upper echelons of the community is an even greater challenge. You must accept what time and energy they can volunteer, for each has their own families and careers. You must meet each member exactly where they are and take what each has to offer and maximize the relationship. This is a very intense undertaking when you are not handing anyone a paycheck each week, and you are not getting paid yourself. The lack of money to motivate the efforts of the individuals can make leading a nonprofit organization much more challenging than leading a for-profit organization, but it also makes the rewards even greater because you do the job well with such* *limited resources. The lack of resources forces a leader in a community-based national nonprofit organization to rely heavily on the quality of their relationships within and outside the organization. It is so easy for one to come up with excuses when you don't have a paycheck to hold over them. Everyone must believe in your leadership to show up and give great effort year after year. The role of great leadership is not to stress and break the system but to provide the system with the necessary strength, energy, passion, and respect to motivate and inspire everyone involved to give their absolute best.*

At Walmart, I recall everyone was always stressed—over the sales numbers, over how the store looked for customers, and over poor employee attendance. No one was ever satisfied, just stressed. While stressing to be better day after day can be an intense part of doing business, mission-driven leadership intensity drives greatness, while arbitrary stress pushes people out. Great leaders are never satisfied with today's level of success in the workplace. They are always striving to improve their own performance and the performance of their team. Great leaders build a mindset into the team that pushes the team to improve day-to-day and year after year; not to push people out of the company, just as we push everyone to be successful within the family at home, not out. Great leaders measure performance and believe the results are a practical, brutally honest assessment of themselves and their team's performance. The results are utilized to motivate and inspire; not to stress. One reason a family member reaches their peak is because other family members are willing to be brutally honest with their assessments. Another reason is that we never want to disappoint our family, so we never stop giving our best. By identifying strengths and weaknesses, great leaders seek to strengthen their strengths and weaken their weaknesses. They constantly

PRINCIPLE SIX: INTENSITY

assess, evaluate, and develop plans to overcome organizational and individual challenges. When we survey the best teams anywhere, like NBA or NFL Teams, they are incessantly intent on adding capability and pushing for higher standards in team and individual performance. You cannot lead out of fear. Fear only causes stress and never produces peak performance. High performance starts with intense leadership and spreads to each of the team members until it becomes the culture, the new standard for greatness; after all, greatness is what greatness does. Greatness is a championship NBA or NFL team because winning an NBA championship is what greatness does. Greatness is a top-performing Fortune 500 company, a well-operating state government, or a nonprofit of community excellence because that is what greatness does. Great leaders produce greatness. Great leaders acknowledge that there are no bad teams but that there are bad leaders who facilitate the bad performance of the team. Likewise, there are no bad children, just bad parenting. Like parenting, leadership is intense! Intense leadership is required to build high-performing teams and enable individuals to strive for a higher standard in self-discipline and personal capacity. Motivation is not the key to producing great teams; intensity is. And intensity has no substitute. Leadership must be intense for the team to succeed, and great leadership is greatly intense. It is this intensity that makes leading others the most challenging and, therefore, the most gratifying of all human endeavors. It gets intense when a child experiences a failure for the first time and you as the parent must build the confidence in your child to keep them excited about tomorrow. It is intense when a spouse is laid off or doesn't get the job promotion they worked so hard for. It is intense when illness visits the family, or a disagreement occurs, or a challenge of the heart causes discourse. Great leadership comes from being always engaged and pushing everyone around you to give you maximum performance every day. Motivation comes and goes. No one is always motivated to give their best. That's not humanly possible. Life comes at us all in various manners that are designed to knock us off our square. Staying on your square is an intense endeavor. Staying poised when employees demonstrate poor attendance or mediocre performance is challenging when you are thriving to succeed with subpar support. The exceptional leader must stand in the face of adversity and display the ability to move his or her team beyond the challenges. If great leadership could be purchased at Walmart or Amazon, then everyone would be a great leader. Unfortunately, intensity is not a top-selling consumer product. Intensity is an intuitive by-product of one's innate ability and pure doggedness in the face of challenge. Intensity is fully understanding the task at hand and committing to developing the discipline and capacity necessary to turn your team of individuals into champions of their industry. Intensity produces greatness, and greatness produces champions.

Imagine you have the pleasure of meeting three NBA players. All three are the leading scorers on their respective teams. You ask all three, "What do you do for your team?" The first player says he is the best shooter on his team and tries to score as many points as possible for his team. The second player answers that he is the best shooter on his team and does his part to help his team win games. The third player conveys that he is the best teammate on his team, and he does everything possible to help his team win championships. Which player would you like to coach? The next day, you are walking into a cathedral. You notice three bricklayers repairing a damaged exterior wall.

You ask all three, "What are you doing?" The first worker says he is laying bricks. The second worker says he is repairing the damaged wall. The third worker responds that he is rebuilding the cathedral. Which worker would you like on your team?

Exercise:
Ask three individuals in your organization the following questions:

1. What is the mission of the organization?
2. What is the vision of the organization's leader?
3. What do you do for your organization?

The answers to these three questions are the practical, brutally honest, and accurate measures of your leadership intensity. Are you producing high-performing champions and institution builders who are mission-driven, or are you managing a team of individuals who are disengaged from the goals and objectives of the organization? Expect and believe the grade you receive. If you are unsatisfied with your grade, then lead with more intensity toward established goals and objectives that are mission-driven and guided by love and affection. Do not forget the love and affection. It works at home, and it will work in the workplace. The exceptional leader must be the driving force that produces high-performing teams and maximum organizational performance at every level within the organization. A leader cannot, without having detrimental effects on the overall outcome, delegate their responsibility to be the driving force of the organization.

When I assumed the leadership roles of director of facilities, maintenance, and operations at various school districts in the state of California, I took the leadership reins of poorly performing departments in poorly performing organizations. I was much younger then and full of energy and oozing with talent and intellect. In each endeavor, I quickly assessed the current performance level, and I believed the results were brutally honest and accurate. The initial analyses were the very crux from which I would move the departments forward. I then performed a market analysis of world-class facilities, maintenance, and operations organizations and established some basic performance goals. The organizations were dismal in comparison to where we needed to be. Most technicians in these departments were severely underperforming and lacked motivation and inspiration to do better. There were no job performance standards. Records showed that one electrician was completing 15 work orders a month on average, and another electrician was completing 90 work orders a month on average. Both electricians had received satisfactory performance evaluations in the last five years, despite their disparaging and varying levels of job performance. The two public school departments historically had been poorly supervised. I am African American and was in charge. The workforce was predominantly non-ethnic White Americans. Thus, I faced extreme levels of racial tension. At one school district, while turning the department around, the team would often show their affection for me be writing the word "NIGGER" on the walls near my office. I inherited departments dominated by good ole boys who were not accustomed to working very hard or being directed by firm leadership hands that belonged to an African American man of extreme abilities. I recognized going in that leading in these environments was going to be extremely challenging. Fortunately, I had some previous experience leading as the first African American to lead departments in the Naval Nuclear Reactor program. I led

PRINCIPLE SIX: INTENSITY

electrical operations as a very young man in the nuclear reactor plants onboard the U.S.S. Enterprise and other naval vessels, directing all the electrical operations of eight nuclear reactors in four plants. I was always the only minority in my department throughout my naval career. I was also always the most capable of everyone in the group. One must be when one is Black or Brown in this country. Extreme challenges require extreme leadership intensity if you intend to be highly successful. In the school districts, as in the Navy, I did not lead with the strong, forceful, and energetic leader that I am by nature. Instead, I led first with love, affection, passion, and understanding—the values I learned from my family. I had to get to know my team and their individual perspectives, abilities, nuances, emotions, and desires. I needed to learn what motivated and inspired each technician. I had to establish some common goals and a common ground. So, I did what every great leader does. I took them fishing! Yes! I took them fishing. We caught fish and talked about our personal lives, and we talked about the mission of the departments and what aspired us to do the work that we do. I allowed them to get to know me, and I learned a lot about who they were. I laid the foundation for a love ethic upon which we could build trust and understanding. I made my role clear and my expectations even clearer. We laughed, joked, and bonded. The next day, I set some basic parameters and established some initial performance goals. I told them that everyone willing to give me good effort would always have a place in my heart and in my department. I also told them that anyone not willing to give me good effort would not find my style of leadership favorable. For a subsequent period, I would just watch, learn, and build relationships. After building relationships, I held group meetings and introduced the teams to the extremely intense strength, force, energy, and feelings I brought to the job. Some things worked, and some did not. Most of the employees in the departments listened and believed I was who I said I was, and there were some who did not listen or believe. Most of the support staff and technicians rose to the occasion, and a few did not. I fired the few, and with extreme leadership intensity, I produced high-performing facilities, maintenance, and operations teams within a year. I led with love and supported my efforts with strength, force, energy, passion, and commitment. I pushed two different groups in intensely challenging situations toward greatness. *Greatness Is What Greatness Does!*

A Leadership Performance Perspective: *Successfully leading a group of five or so individuals can be a very intense endeavor. Everyone must succeed so the team can succeed. Success depends on each person doing their part in a manner that supports the team's success. If I am part of a group of six, my success is dependent on the actions of the other five. I have five dependent events that must occur precisely in alignment with the common goals and objectives. Creating the workplace environment that provides for such alignment is the key role and responsibility of leadership. The senior leadership, supported by the human resources department, must take full responsibility for the organization's culture, and leadership must be a partner to every employee in creating the culture. Serving as a leader in the workplace and leading a team of 5–6, 100, 40,000, or two million individuals is an intense undertaking. Let me add here that leading more than 10 direct reports is more than most humans can successfully lead and lead well. In the workplace, you do not have the intrinsic benefit of love and affection toward your subordinates, and you do not naturally have the outward pleasure of being loved by your subordinates. Creating the culture for such a love*

PRINCIPLE SIX: INTENSITY

ethic to be established can only happen over time and with human resources and leadership acting in partnership. In senior leadership roles, I worked diligently and intensely to create the appropriate culture so that everyone in the company felt that they were valued and cared for. At times, I dealt with other senior leadership refusing to do their part and partner with the programs and processes I attempted to establish. As a result of senior leadership refusing to personally engage the culture and delegating the function of making everyone feel loved to the HR role, no one in one company I worked for felt that senior management cared about them. There were very few good relationships between senior management and hourly staff in the field. The company could not keep critical employees for any affective amount of time. Most junior architects and project leads left for other design firms. This company is now out of business. Going out of business is the result of leadership that refuses to engage and connect with a culture of caring. This is why the previously discussed Principle 2 on relationships is so critical to creating an environment in the workplace that provides for the development of trusting and loving relationships between the leader and his or her subordinates. No amount of leadership intensity can overcome bad relationships in the workplace. If you believe leading 6–10 people as a supervisor is intense, try leading 20–30 as a manager, 50–75 as a director, or even 200+ as part of senior management in charge of an entire division. Imagine being in charge of the 40,000 plus officers employed by the New York City Police Department. Imagine leading a company as large as Walmart. Leadership intensity grows as the size of your group grows and as your level of responsibilities increase, if you are a leader intent on building high-performing teams. Your level of intensity is your level of energy available for a particular task you need to complete, and intense energy is required to reach high altitudes in leadership performance.

PRINCIPLE SEVEN

People, Processes, and Paradigms

People, Processes, and Paradigms: The Exceptional leader creates performance paradigms with exceptional people and processes in mind.

> *"In order to reach your leadership evolution, you must first go through a personal revolution, which comes from an intense professional involution."*
>
> —Ronald T. Hickey

A paradigm is a model or pattern for something that may be copied or repeated to establish a process for success or identify the reason for process failure. A paradigm is also described as a theory or a group of ideas concerning how something should be done, made, or thought about, again to establish a process for success or identify the reason for process failure. A paradigm allows the leader and his or her team to evaluate their performance, self-diagnose the reason they may have failed, and determine what needs to change, a paradigm shift, to produce a successful process. In producing a paradigm, the goal should be to analyze the sophisticated failures of people so that a more simplified process can evolve to revolutionize the success for your people. Or, as Ronald T. Hickey states,

PRINCIPLE SEVEN: PEOPLE, PROCESSES, AND PARADIGMS

"In order to get to your evolution, you must first go through a revolution, which comes from an involution." Understanding why you succeed and why you fail are critically important to being able to create processes, patterns, and models that can be copied to create workplace environments where success and high performance can be systemically repeated. The goal in creating paradigms in the workplace is to create a theoretical framework, a paradigm of sort, within which an organization can study and formulate answers to problems that adversely affect its performance. The paradigm will provide a foundation of intrinsic critical thinking that will assist in identifying core problems resulting from the imbalance in functional processes and team environments produced as a result of dependent events and statistical fluctuations. The resultant paradigm will identify the issue, produce the answer, create the new environment, and determine necessary actions and resources, the paradigm shift, that must occur to reach a resolution to routine failures and low performance. Resolve should be self-liberating, and the proper paradigm will get you there.

Exercise: The Hoola Hoop Paradigm

Step 1: The facilitator places a large hoola hoop on the floor. You can purchase these at any store that sells children's toys. Selected the largest hoola hoop and select the one that is lightweight.

Step 2: Randomly select six members of your team or audience and have them stand spread evenly apart around the hoola hoop. Once spread evenly apart, have each participant stand back approximately 12" from the hoola hoop that should still be on the floor.

Step 3: Give the participants three rules. Each member must follow the three rules at all times, or the team has failed to complete the task.
> Rule 1: Hold both hands out with their fists clutched and only their two index fingers extended. Their index fingers and fists must remain in this orientation at all times.
> Rule 2: The hoola hoop will be placed on top of the 12 extended index fingers. The hoola hoop must remain on top and in contact with ALL 12 index fingers at all times. Remember Rule 1. The index fingers cannot be hooked around the hoola hoop or changed to any other orientation. No index finger can become disconnected from the hoola hoop. If so, the team fails.
> Rule 3: Lower the hoola hoop to the floor. The hoola hoop must remain on top and touching all 12 index fingers always as the hoola hoop is lowered to the ground.

Step 4: Repeat Step 3 as many times as necessary until all participants understand the rules.

Step 5: The facilitator raises the hoola hoop to the eye level of the tallest participant and instructs all participants to raise their indexes fingers until all 12 index fingers are touching the hoola hoop.

Step 6: The facilitator instructs the six participants to lower the hoola hoop to the floor while following the three rules listed in Step 3. It is crucial that you give no additional instructions at this point. The facilitator lets go of the hoola hoop and says, "GO!"

Step 7: The facilitator monitors the exercise to ensure no index finger becomes disconnected or changes orientation. If either happens, the facilitator instructs the team they have failed, and they must start over.

PRINCIPLE SEVEN: PEOPLE, PROCESSES, AND PARADIGMS

If all steps have been followed correctly, something amazing and equally comical should happen! The group should flail like crazy, the hoola hoop should be all over the place, and fingers should be off the hoola hoop!! The group will fail miserably. The amazing part will be the group's ability to clearly identify why they failed so miserably. What they identify will be their paradigm. Here are the top 10 reasons groups of this exercise will list as their reasons for failing:

1. No leadership
2. Poor communication
3. No plan of action
4. Lack of full understanding of the task
5. Lack of trust
6. Fear of failure
7. Different perspectives
8. Poor relationships with other team members
9. Different levels of abilities
10. Too many chiefs and not enough Indians

The reason this list is amazing is that every item on it is identical to reasons identified in the workplace for teams failing to complete basic, routine, simple, and/or complex exercises. The team items listed make up the paradigm. The leader and his or her team must now create the paradigm shift for success. Thus, the paradigm shift would be as follows:

Paradigm
1. No Leadership
2. Poor communication

Paradigm Shift
1. Chose a leader
2. Excellent communication

3. No plan of action	3. Develop a plan
4. Lack of understanding	4. Instruct and train
	5. Build trust
5. Lack of trust	6. Create an inclusive culture
6. Fear of failure	7. Understand everyone is different
7. Different perspectives	
	8. Conduct team-building exercises
8. Poor relationships	
9. Different levels of abilities	9. Cross train
	10. Define roles and responsibilities
10. Too many chiefs	

Step 8: Create the paradigm shift and repeat Steps 5–7. Inform the team that the three basic rules should not be allowed to limit what they can do. Instruct the team there are many things that can be done while keeping all 12 fingers at the proper orientation and in contact with the hoola hoop always.

Step 9: Create a new paradigm.

Step 10: Create a new paradigm shift and repeat Steps 5–7.

The team should "fail better" each time. By failing better, the team demonstrates that by creating a paradigm and the paradigm shift, they can create a model or pattern for something that may be copied or repeated to establish a process for success or identify the reason for process failure. The team members demonstrate that they understand the theory or a group of ideas concerning how something should be done, made, or thought about to establish a process for success or identify the reason for process failure. They demonstrate that they can create paradigms that will drive them to become high-performing successful teams as long as they build upon the patterns, models, and processes for success.

The Hoola Hoop Paradigm is a practical science of developing process patterns and critical thinking that establishes a framework for individuals, companies, and organizations developing understanding of the human dynamics associated with managing change, building productive team environments, and driving people to achieve unprecedented levels of performance. It is an incredibly powerful tool because it challenges you at the core of your basic beliefs and allows you to identify and develop a complete understanding of the two universal phenomena—**Dependent Events** and **Statistical Fluctuations**—that affect individual and team performances within an organization. By understanding the significance of the two universal phenomena on human behavior and action, you will learn how the perceptions, feelings, thoughts, ideas, motivations, and actions of employees within your organization affect your company's bottom line. The use of paradigms develops people through the development of effective and professional self-awareness, communication, leadership, trust, respect, and cooperation and provides the necessary framework for people solving their own problems with change management, performance, and team-building issues by deploying concepts associated with creative imagination and critical thinking. Creating workplace paradigms for success will consistently deliver positive and intended results regardless of the task at hand.

Dependent Events: When working in a group or team setting, each member must depend on all others in the group or on the team to perform in a manner that will result in success of the group or team. In the hoola hoop exercise, each person depends on all others keeping their index finger in physical contact with the hoola hoop. Each person is dependent on all others lowering the hoola hoop at the appropriate rate and in the appropriate manner, as expected by every team member. With six participants, each person has five dependent events. Every movement of all six team members must be perfectly synchronized. One movement can only be successful if the other five movements are properly executed. If one person moves the hoola hoop down too slow or too fast, the result is that fingers will become disconnected, and the team fails. Each team member needs the other five team members to perform according to their individual and collective expectations. This is precisely the universal phenomenon of dependent events in group dynamics. To further express this theory, instruct two individuals to complete the hoola hoop exercise. The group will learn that two individuals are more successful at the hoola hoop exercise because less dependent events are involved. Hence, often times, less is better because you have fewer perspectives, variances, ideas, and emotions to consider.

Statistical Fluctuations: No one performs exactly the same every day. Our performances fluctuate. Our actions, movements, patterns, and processes fluctuate daily. That is why performances are averaged out. A person can typically be counted on to perform at an average rate. Life happens, and employees bring their lives into the workplace—problems at home, death in the family, stress, and worry. All these human emotions have an effect on performance that guarantees that performance statistically fluctuates. These fluctuations guarantee that teams will fail if statistical fluctuations are not factored into plans, processes, and procedures. Statistical fluctuations are the very reason having a proven process that produces repeated success is crucial. In sports competitions, a player's average is the focus because a specific performance cannot be guaranteed from game to game. While a basketball player may score 30 points one game, they cannot be depended on to score exactly 30 points every game. The team expects the player to score their average.

Let's Bake Some Oatmeal Raisin Cookies

I am an excellent cook. Many have experienced and rave about my skills in the kitchen. When cooking, the recipe and the discipline to follow instructions and processes become critical to producing great dishes that are consistently delicious. Therefore, we can learn much about the practical aspects of leadership in the kitchen. For instance, I have learned that being an exceptional leader can be compared to baking oatmeal raisin cookies from scratch. It all starts with a great recipe and a proven process for making great cookies every time. You first decide that you want to make some oatmeal raisin cookies—that's the task at hand. Then, you prepare the kitchen. You preheat the oven and retrieve all the necessary bowls, pans, utensils, and whatever you need to be successful. Then you gather the ingredients. You get the flour, yeast, vegetable oil, butter, eggs, salt, sugar, oatmeal, raisins, extract, and baking soda. Now, if you have never made cookies from scratch before, you may have only an idea of what you should do with the ingredients. If you endeavor to make those cookies from scratch without someone properly guiding you through the process, the cookies could become a disaster. You must know the right temperature for the oven. You must know the right measurement for each of the ingredients because too much or too little of any one ingredient will significantly affect the taste, texture, and quality of the cookies. Thus, the recipe (the process) is critical. You must know how long to let the cookies bake. You must know that the oatmeal and raisins should be soaked in water before you place them in the cookie mix so that the cookies will be moist and chewy. If you don't soak the oatmeal and raisins in water first, they will absorb too much moisture from the mix and the cookies will come out dry and brittle. So, there is no way a person can make tasteful and chewy oatmeal raisin cookies from scratch without first being properly coached, mentored, taught, or guided through the process several times before a solo attempt is made. And when your oatmeal raisin cookies from scratch come out perfect and great, the end product is a testament to the leadership and commitment to the performance paradigm that was involved. Whoever created the recipe, overtime, made changes that resulted in the exact recipe being utilized. They deployed a paradigm of sorts until they produced a recipe that produced the desired oatmeal raisin cookie. Your output at work is just like those cookies. How the workplace evolves is predicated on the paradigm, process, and recipe you utilize. Exceptional leadership will ensure the right process. As a great leader, you grow in your career and collect everything you need to be successful. At some point, you have all the ingredients to be as highly successful as you desire, but you may not know how to measure out just the right amount of ingredients to make your leadership taste right to everyone around you. You may not know the correct temperature for all your given situations, conditions, and circumstances. You may not know that some ingredients need special preparation before being added to the mix, like the raisins and the oatmeal being soaked in water.

There is a tremendous amount of knowledge and skill required to become extraordinarily successful, and if you are fortunate, others in your life have invested and contributed in a manner that delivers you with everything you need to have the life you want and the leadership you thrive for. Develop the ability to create paradigms that enable you to determine what is missing in your recipe or process. Hire the absolute best collection of talent possible, and your oatmeal raisin cookies will come out perfect each and every time! I know that leadership endeavors may appear oversimplified at times, just as baking cookies may seem, as you are tempted to engage in some activities without fully knowing what it takes to be successful. Paradigms will lead, inform, guide, and coach you along your path to success.

Explore *The 10 Challenges of the Hoola Hoop Paradigm* to see how this unique, perpetual methodology will provide you with a framework for challenging employees, managing change, and increasing the performance and achievement of your employees in both their personal lives and professional endeavors.

When challenging employees, teammates, or peers to reach higher levels of performance, having a process is very important for the team leader and the team players. Coaching peak performance using the Hoola Hoop Paradigm is a very different process. Critical thinking is an extremely powerful part of successfully implementing the Hoola Hoop Paradigm to realize the desired achievement. The coach's role is more of a professional assertion—directing thought patterns, leading the way to the path to critical thinking, and creating processes for successful execution of plans. Having the employees and players on the team understand the steps of the processes is also very important. Deploying a shared process is critical to creating a common language and an appreciation for the patterns and paths of the journey ahead. Here are the 10 challenges of the Hoola Hoop Paradigm:

1. **Discover Who You Are:** Self-discovery is real power in learning to become a team player and a team leader. Lack of self-knowledge limits your ability to determine your individual ambitions and how you can best serve on the team. Knowledge gives you information. Information can be shared. If there is no pertinent information you can share with your team about yourself, you may want to reassess your ability to support the goals of the team. Something about your person (talents, ambitions, and visions) must align with the vision of the team for you to be of positive assistance to the team. Discovering who you are is the purpose of the exercises in Principle 1 on perspectives. Who you are at the molecular level, or quantum level, matters. You and your team members' perspective will have an effect on everything you do.

2. **Identify Your Ambitions and the Ambitions of the Team:** Ambitions create a strong desire to achieve something. Sharing ambitions between the team leader and the team players helps establish an atmosphere for trusting teamwork and achieving success. It also allows the team to assess if there is a common purpose among the team that is in complete alignment with the ambitions of the individuals and visions of the organization. In essence, identifying ambitions determines if there truly is a team. Teammates must have a common goal and a common interest in reaching the goal to be successful as a team.

3. **Properly Align and Manage Your Talent Pool with the Overall Vision:** Understanding the abilities and talents of individuals on the team is vital to ensuring you have the

PRINCIPLE SEVEN: PEOPLE, PROCESSES, AND PARADIGMS

ability to properly align talent for peak performance. If we are unequivocally aware of the talent pool, we can best deploy our resources for optimum achievement. It also allows us to identify weakness in the talent pool. This knowledge is as important to success as knowing your strengths. In addition, adequate talent management (ensuring every individual is tasked and rewarded in a manner that supports their individual ambitions and team's ambitions) is the sure way to talent retention and recruitment. Talent, ambition, and vision must be aligned for success.

4. **Create a Framework for Critical Thinking:** Critical thinking will produce new perceptions and new ideas. Perception defines our vision and desire for something. Perceptions generate all our thoughts and feelings. Ideas motivate us to action. With new perceptions and fresh ideas, we step in the direction of success and unprecedented achievement. Furthermore, and perhaps most importantly, a solid framework for critical thinking eliminates the dependency on others to solve your every problem. If an organization constantly employs outside consultants to come in and figure out what is wrong, then the organization needs to reassess its talent pool for strengths and weaknesses.

5. **Develop Process Patterns for Success:** Process patterns can ensure you are either consistently successful or consistently unsuccessful. The goal should be to develop process patterns that are proven to deliver success. Failure will simply happen from time to time; no process pattern can guarantee peak performance 100% of the time. But proven patterns will increase your success rate to a predictable level. Process patterns, not individual errors or successes, are the keys to a successful journey. The goal in developing

patterns is to ensure that you are not carrying errors forward and that your process delivers desired results each and every time. Additionally, process patterns will negate weaknesses in your talent pool. Understand that the true genius is the software architect that created the software program, not the end user who simply masters the utilization of the program. Allow great process patterns to be the architect of your business and operations strategies, and performance will reach levels well beyond your current abilities.

6. **Understand What Works and Why It Works:** Once process patterns are developed that deliver desired results every time, you should initially study the reasons the patterns are successful or effective. You can eliminate mistakes by sticking to what you fully understand. Focusing on what you know provides an atmosphere of confidence in your work and promotes a foundation for growth. You cannot get better at something until you understand what you are doing right and why you are doing it right. Without understanding this, success is only a matter of luck, and failure is simply a matter of time.

7. **Understand What Does Not Work and Why It Does Not Work:** Understand what patterns are not working and why they are not working. Positive continuous growth quarter after quarter and year after year cannot occur until obstacles to pattern developing are eliminated. Understanding what does not work and why it does not work will also prevent carrying errors forward. Failure to understand what does not work and why it does not work is the very reason organizations waste time, resources, and energy trying to get different results with the same old processes. Albert Einstein once stated that "The definition of insanity is

doing the same thing over and over but expecting different results." Organizational insanity is the result of not understanding why something does not work, so you keep doing it regardless.

8. **Trust in Your Own Abilities and the Abilities of Your Teammates:** If you cannot trust your own abilities or the abilities of your teammates to think critically to bring resolve to fundamental problems in your process patterns, you will never reach your full potential, and your team will never experience the success that only comes from interdependency. There are only a few things that are more counterproductive to success within a teamwork atmosphere than a person who does not trust their teammates. Have you ever noticed the difference in NBA Superstars LeBron James, Steph Curry, or Kevin Durant when they played with teammates they trusted as opposed to teammates they did not trust? Just like NBA superstars, if you trust your teammates, your individual statistics will decrease, but the team's success rate increases. And vice versa, if you do not trust your teammates, your individual statistics increase, but the team's success rate decreases. I would say, beyond a shadow of a doubt, that trusting in your abilities and the abilities of your teammates are synonymous with a high success rate of any team in any organization.

9. **Learn From Your Experiences:** The process patterns must be examined! Experience allows learning from the execution of the process. Grade the process fairly and trust the process based on the grade. Learn from both your mistakes and your successes. Mastering this challenge is paramount for developing trust in your abilities and the abilities of your teammates. If you cannot accurately examine and

grade your own work, then it becomes essentially impossible to establish the degree of your abilities in reference to the full potential of the process. Socrates once stated that "The unexamined life was not worth living." In an organizational setting, the unexamined process is worthless to your business. You simply must learn from your experiences, successes, and failures. If you fail to do so, you are just going through the motions, like so many businesses, teams, and individuals.

10. **Understand that Greatness Must Be Coached:** Every organization should instinctively understand that talent alone will not harness success, no matter the level of ambition and talent. Every great team, every single one of them, has had or has a great coach that coached the great ambitions and talents on the team to success and ultimate championships. Even the world's greatest golfer, Tiger Woods, with all his talent and ambition has a swing coach. If Tiger Woods understands that he needs a great coach so that he can be great at golf, shouldn't all organizations embrace the fact that they need a great coach if they are to be great in the sports of business?

More information on these 10 challenges and their proper implementation, application, and examples can be found in Ron Hickey's book, *The Hoola Hoop Paradigm: Are You Up for the Challenge? Become as Great as You Want to Be.*

A Leadership Performance Perspective: Being able to create a paradigm for success is vital to exceptional leadership. Patterns and models for success are a collection of proven techniques and theories that changes the way your organization will interact, communicate,

PRINCIPLE SEVEN: PEOPLE, PROCESSES, AND PARADIGMS

operate, and cooperate with one another. Paradigms are not the typical top-down style of leadership. The Hoola Hoop Paradigm engages all employees at all rungs of the ladder in your organization. Paradigms are a concept based on communication, critical thinking, and action from everyone. If organizations desire to improve, they can only do so by empowering the entire organization to communicate better, think better, and operate better. How does an organization mold an entire enterprise by allowing only a select few to obtain training? The answer is that the organization does not. Organizations must ignite the flame within every employee to perform at their very best. The Hoola Hoop Paradigm provides such an ignition. The incitement to succeed must be an internal and personal psychology that is from within and emits outward. The Hoola Hoop Paradigm is a framework that will help your organization consistently achieve its desired business results while developing its employees to be incited and self-actualized.

Here is an example of why the Hoola Hoop Paradigm works: Let's say that I want to help a team of individuals identify their efficiencies and inefficiencies in teamwork. I could elect to do one of the following:

1. Discipline members of the team every time the team fails.
2. Constantly watch over the team so that the team never fails.
3. Subject the team to an exercise that demonstrates they are functioning poorly as a team and then guide them through team exercises that allow them to develop their own processes for success.

In the **first scenario,** the team learns that making a mistake produces a negative disciplinary action. Thus, they will be very careful and timid. They will refuse to think outside the box to come up with new ideas for success. The possibility of making a mistake may terrify them so much that the team never employs critical thinking and creative imagination. Negative reinforcement puts out the flames of excellence and tethers your organization in depths of mediocrity and fear.

In the **second scenario**, the organization is promoting dependence. The organization feels safe only when the team is being told exactly what, when, who, why, and how to perform a task. When the team finds itself without the guidance of its overseer, it will become unproductive until the overseer returns. The team will never learn to think for itself or perform at its peak level. This team will only go as far as its dictator can take them and will never benefit from the collective intelligence of the group. Dependence is crippling.

In the **third scenario**, the team will learn from experience what works and what does not work. In this process, the team will also understand why something works and why it does not work. Understanding why will exist as the framework for developing answers through the critical thinking process. Creative imagination will be developed, and self-actualization will drive the team to new levels of success. Quality communication will be garnered, and ideas from the individual critical thinkers will be encouraged. The flame of excellence will be fueled by goal achievements. This will be a high-performing team. This team will birth new leaders of the organization.

The Hoola Hoop Paradigm operates in the third scenario above. That is why it works. A simple hoola hoop exercise is utilized to demonstrate the reasons why a team experiences failure, primarily due to poor communication. The hoola hoop exercise also identifies the answers to the problems presented by human

PRINCIPLE SEVEN: PEOPLE, PROCESSES, AND PARADIGMS

factors in team environments. Then, group critical thinking exercises are deployed to assist the team in developing process patterns to guide them down the path to better communication skills and higher success rates. The exercises are simple and can be completed in only a few minutes each day. The exercises produce more answers each time the exercises are conducted. The Hoola Hoop Paradigm has infinite potential. The science driving the paradigm is only limited by the individuals of the team and their understanding and willingness to address the human effects of **Dependent Events** and **Statistical Fluctuations** on their personal and professional lives. So, what is the "secret" to the Hoola Hoop Paradigm? There is no secret. The paradigm simply incites the entire organization to process new theories and develop an internal ambition to achieve absolute greatness and helps everyone understand that greatness is simply a matter of choice. And this is accomplished through the study and continual use of this practical science.

A Leadership Development Perspective: As an exceptional leader, you must be prepared to become an invaluable member of your organization. If you do so, you will inspire success and high levels of performance. The theories embedded in the Hoola Hoop Paradigm will produce five critical thinking processes for your leadership and your organization:

1. **Provide a Proven Process for Delivering Desired Results:** As an exceptional leader, you will do more than just energize employees with the recanting of great success stories. Paradigms present a simple, detailed, and clear process that has been proven to produce desired results and process patterns for success. Examined process patterns will

establish the solid foundation of repeated success upon which high levels of performance can be realized on a continuous basis. Process patterns are the cornerstones of success and building high performance. Employees need tangibles that can be deployed daily. There must be a road map for deploying those tangibles. Not everyone can be like Mike (Michael Jordan), but everyone can implement a proven process and obtain desired results. The Hoola Hoop Paradigm will deliver proven and repeatable processes of patterns to deliver success constantly and continually. The Hoola Hoop Paradigm will help your organization find success in your goals.

2. **Focus on Team Building by First Focusing on the Ambitions of Each Player:** As an exceptional leader, you must provide a team atmosphere and deliver a message that encourages the individual ambitions of each member of your organization. Not everyone wants to be the CEO of the company, but some do harbor such ambitions. Some people want to be brain surgeons, others want to be the lead singer in a rock band, while others may have personal goals that are not so lofty. The point is that everyone has ambition, and everyone's ambition should be known and considered in a team environment. No one should feel as if their goals are insignificant. The ability to incite everyone on an individual level to achieve high performance will make your leadership more personal and goals more achievable. The first focus of team building is to have every member of the team achieve something that they previously thought was impossible or too difficult to attempt. The next focus will be to encourage the entire team to accomplish a single organizational goal. To incite a group of

PRINCIPLE SEVEN: PEOPLE, PROCESSES, AND PARADIGMS

individuals to successfully focus on their individual ambitions and to equally incite the group to find success as a unit is simply "extraordinary." That is the very juncture at which the Hoola Hoop Paradigm supports the creation of high-performing organizations.

3. **Challenge Each Player to Become Self-Actualized:** Self-actualization is the combination of the organization and the individual employee producing the proper motivation and attitude for high performance. A self-actualized employee is self-motivated in their role in the organization and reports to work with the proper attitude for a successful day. They are excited each morning about the prospect of reporting to work and playing an important role in the organization's success. They develop ideas through critical thinking and need no supervision, just a process. They are prone to excellence, and failure is not an option. Your organization's corporate culture will benefit most from your ability to inspire your employees to be self-actualized. There is a tremendous delta between motivating an employee with professional incentives and inspiring people to be self-actualized for the rest of their lives. Self-actualization is addictive and contagious. A corporate culture where employees are inspired to inspire excellence in each other is beyond reproach. The Hoola Hoop Paradigm will provide such inspiration of excellence.

4. **Motivate Players to Align Their Talents with the Goals of the Organization:** Talent alone does not ensure success or achievement. For an organization to experience the success of its goals, the talent of all its players must be properly aligned with the goals of the organization. The Hoola Hoop Paradigm will vividly show your employees what can

be achieved when they unite behind your company's vision. The paradigm will also show why misalignment of talent to the company's vision presents a formidable challenge to the company achieving success and high performance. Moreover, it will demonstrate to your organization exactly how to incite your employees to help your organization reach your strategic goals. This is a primary objective of the exceptional leader. The ability to move an entire organization to support one vision while encouraging each employee to embrace their personal visions and values is a unique ability that is very attainable with the theories your organization will discover through the practical science of creating paradigms.

5. **Provide Practical Exercises that Produce Peak Performances:** Paradigms provide a process for (or at least informs) a continuous improvement program to reinforce and develop more advanced concepts. This program may include seminars and workshops with all employees (especially leaders and mid-management), additional training, and coaching on an individual basis. This process provides practical exercises that can be conducted at any level and with any number of employees. These tangible and practical exercises are essential as you encourage the vision and ambition of each individual to achieve lasting personal and professional growth and peak performance. Motivation tends to be a fleeting emotional high that lasts for only a moment. Achieving lasting levels of high performance through the encouragement of personal vision and ambition is an intrinsically powerful mindset that will last the entire journey. Practical exercises like the Hoola Hoop Paradigm provide such mindsets.

In addition to the above five critical thinking processes, the success of your organization will also depend on the longevity of the mindsets for achievement developed with the practical exercises. There are three reasons your organization will remain incited to achieve success and increase its longevity for success and high performance:

1. **A Proven Process:** A proven process provides a common path, pattern, language and environment for organizations to achieve the full fruition of their stated goals and visions. The Hoola Hoop Paradigm will provide such a process that can be practically applied daily. A process also provides for establishing evaluation parameters by which an organization can measure how far it has traveled down the path to success.
2. **Creating Performance Paradigms:** Sustained success can only occur after hours and hours of training and creating performance paradigms. Performance paradigms provide ongoing support and leadership development that reinforce all the training provided. Sustained performance management requires constant encouragement and continuous coaching.
3. **High Achievement Support:** Leadership must be practical in its expectations. Goals should be attainable and should require exertion at every aspect of the process. The vision of the leadership should recognize those individuals or groups that are responding to the needs of the organization to change and develop successfully. Leadership must support achievement. Priorities of leadership must include continual employee development and coaching to prevent employees from losing the incitement

established by the Hoola Hoop Paradigm. The paradigm's performance coaching guides leadership through the process of achievement support. Achievement is built upon achievement. Success is built upon success. Both must be supported to ensure that both are sustainable within the organization.

Are you ready to embark upon a new path to success and to increasing your organization's performance? If so, then the time has come for you to look closer at the Hoola Hoop Paradigm—a proven concept for enhancing performance and managing change that integrates critical thinking skills and powerful nuances. The time has also come for your management team to communicate to your entire organization that *Greatness Is What Greatness Does.*"

Exercise: Hoola Hoop Paradigm Revised

Complete Steps 1–6 in the Hoola Hoop Paradigm exercise above. But this time, use only two participants. You will discover that two people can complete the exercise successfully the first time. Now engage your team in discussion and discover all the reasons two can accomplish what six cannot. Understanding these reasons is the bedrock of exceptional leadership.

Understand What Does Not Work and Why

"The relationship between "what is right" and "what is wrong" is so fragile that one wrong act can completely obliterate a lifetime of success. And afterwards, you may have to spend the rest of your life trying to recover what was lost."
—Ronald T. Hickey

Performance paradigms assist leaders and teams in understanding what does not work and why. The success of your organization, your team, and your leadership depends on you understanding what does not work and why! In the first Hoola Hoop Paradigm exercise, the paradigm created listed why you failed. The second Hoola Hoop Paradigm, with just two participants, helps you understand what does not work and why. Your positive and continuous growth day after day, month after month, quarter after quarter, and year after year cannot and will not occur until obstacles to developing successful patterns are eliminated. Knowing what not to do, and why, is vitally important to this end. Failure to understand what does not work and why it does not work is the very reasons individuals, teams, and organizations waste time, resources, and energy trying to get different results with the same old habits, processes, and traditions. Understanding what does not work and why it does not work is not just simply the opposite of understanding what works and why it works. Understanding one concept does not necessarily mean you understand the other. The two understandings are partners in success, not opposing competitors. Failure to understand what does not work and why it does not work can be counterproductive to success. It is counterproductive to success primarily in two functional areas of success. Keep in mind that there are many functional areas of success. *Time* is the first functional area adversely affected by not understanding what does not work and why. If you expend time engaged in activities that do not work in a particular endeavor, you are wasting valuable time that could be spent engaged in activities that you know will bring you success. You can never recover the time; it is forever lost. Additionally, not understanding why an activity does not work exposes you to the risk of repeating the activities over an expanded period, further wasting valuable time. Wasting time is counterproductive to achieving success because success is often a matter of time and deadlines. *Progression* is the second functional area adversely affected by not understanding why something does not work. Success typically occurs in a progressive manner. We build upon past success to become more successful. Completing tasks that we understand to work in delivering success in a particular endeavor provides for progression toward ultimate organizational goals and individual achievement. But our progress can be minimized, retarded, or nullified by activities that do not work in the particular process or pattern.

> *"Every man is a damn fool for at least five minutes every day; wisdom consists in not exceeding the limit."*
> —Elbert Hubbard

A Leadership Development Perspective: *If we are going to strive to be successful leaders, we must create paradigms that help us understand what does not work in our organizations and why it does not work. We cannot be great contributors on our teams or in our organizations if our actions are counterproductive to the goals of success. If a leader can eliminate the five minutes each day in which they act counterproductively to success, the leader will be successful in providing an atmosphere more congenial for the pursuit of high performance and greatness. To assist in eliminating, or at least not exceeding, the five minutes in my day that can be detrimental to success, I utilized my modification to the Socrates triple filter test. I made some changes to the test because in the Socrates triple filter test, you need only pass one of the three tests. In my test, your words and deeds must pass all three tests. I refer to my test as the positive*

PRINCIPLE SEVEN: PEOPLE, PROCESSES, AND PARADIGMS

outcome performance (POP) test. If your actions are always "beneficial high performance-based positive actions," then your actions should always forward your positive agenda. Essentially, success is promoted by your actions when your actions are high performing, positive, and beneficial—your actions POP! The POP test consists of testing your actions through three questions as tests.

The first test is the high-performance test. Ask yourself, "Does the action demonstrate high performance?" If your answer is no, resist taking action. Your organization, team, coworkers, and associates should be able to trust that your every action intends to be actions that demonstrate high performance. If you do it, it ought to be as good as platinum. One is hard pressed to find anything more counterproductive to success and/or damaging to a person's leadership reputation than being labeled or thought of as a leader who does not perform at a very high level. If you are not sure of your actions, information, and facts, verify your actions, research the information until you are sure, and demonstrate excellence in everything you do. If the action is unequivocally an act of excellence, then proceed to the next test before you follow through with the action.

The second test is the positive test. Ask yourself, "Is the action a positive action?" If the intended action is positive, it should have no negative effects whatsoever. Simply because an action demonstrates high performance does not suggest the action is positive. Gossip, for example, is comprised primarily of factual information about someone but is normally negative in nature. A positive statement should be an utterance that any reasonable person would welcome. Another way to determine if an action is positive is to ask yourself if you would take the action if the CEO, chairman of the board, or your mentee was standing next to you. Remember, actions are like boomerangs;

everything you do comes back to you. If the action is not a positive act, resist taking the action. No one really likes a gossiper, and no one really trusts a person unwilling to stand in front of their action. As the saying goes, "Loose lips sink ships." Actions and words are powerful, whether negative or positive. Now, if the action is a positive action, proceed to the final test before taking the action.

The third and final test is the benefit test. Ask yourself, "Is the action beneficial to the operations of the organization?" Your actions should be something that the organization deems as useful in its efforts to create and build upon success. When your actions are a benefit to the organization, either in word or deed, you are a tremendous and invaluable asset to the overall success of the organization. So, if your actions are high performing, positive, and beneficial, execute them freely and often. Your success and the success of those around you depend on your actions "popping!"

There was once an old peasant who worked the fields for a very rich aristocrat. The peasant figured that the rich aristocrat had more than the aristocrat would ever need. So, he decided that each day, he would take a little grain from the harvest he was employed to take in. He figured the rich aristocrat would never miss the grain if he took just a very small amount each day. The peasant's plan was to save up enough grain to eventually go into business for himself and get rich. One morning, he awoke and noticed the rats had torn into his grain sack and eaten a good portion of the grain he was taking for himself. The peasant decided to tie the grain sack to a rafter in the barn in which he slept. He believed that allowing the sack of grain to hang from the ceiling rafters so the rats could not get to it was a great means of keeping the gain safe from any rats. The peasant also decided to sleep under the sack of grain so he could keep an eye out for rats in the middle of the night. One night, a rat ate through the rope that tied the sack to the rafters. The heavy sack of grain fell and landed directly onto the peasant's head, killing him instantly.

Exceptional leaders must learn to create performance paradigms for creating people's successes and to triple test all actions before executing. If the old peasant in the story above had deployed concepts similar to the concepts of creating paradigms and paradigm shifts or had utilized some version of the triple filter test or POP test, he may have avoided his death in the manner described. Testing your intended actions before taking the actions is as important as creating the paradigms that identify your reasons for failing. Remember, *Greatness Is What Greatness Does.*

PRINCIPLE EIGHT

Leadership

Leadership: The Exceptional leader leads the way by modeling Exceptional Leadership behaviors and skills.

> *"Great leadership is not commanding with authority. Great leadership is the love for people made visible. You cannot lead people if you do not love people, and they have to see and trust that you love them enough to lead them to their success."*
>
> —Ronald T. Hickey

Exceptional leadership must be rooted in a love ethic that ensures others that they can confidently follow you and be led to a destination that is majorly desired. A leader must lead the way to be a leader, and the destination you are encouraging others to follow you to must be a destination that your followers vehemently desire to pursue. The destination is what defines your leadership. If the destination is greatness, then you are a great leader. NFL teams win championships largely because a championship is a destination everyone on the team vehemently desires to pursue. Therefore, every player on a Championship NFL team must be willing to be led toward winning a Superbowl. Every coach in the NFL who has ever won a Superbowl, every last one of them, is considered a great coach because winning a Superbowl is a great pursuit.

PRINCIPLE EIGHT: LEADERSHIP

A championship of some sort, a Superbowl, or a prestigious industry recognition is a desired destination. In the more traditional workplace, the leader must identify the championship that his or her staff is highly interested in being led to win. Jack Welch won championships at General Electric because the destination he chose was the destination his team at GE was interested in following Jack to. Understanding what causes others to want to follow you is starkly different from creating paradigms for developing patterns that are proven to be successful. Paradigms were discussed in the previous principle. Paradigms, patterns, and modalities provide the "how to" step-by-step procedure for accomplishing something or "how to" reach your desired destination with a great deal of consistency and accuracy. Knowing "how to" lead others and understanding "why" others want to follow you afford you the opportunity to truly evaluate the efficiency and productiveness of the details and internal workings of the step-by-step procedures that eventually win championships. While the joy may be in the final product, true love for the work and for those doing the work is developed in the details of knowing "why" others want to follow. An exceptional leader loves what they do and does what they love, all while loving their staff and leading the way to a desired destination.

An exceptional leader leads the way by:

1. Modeling what success looks like
2. Inspiring a common destination
3. Challenging others to maximize performance
4. Empowering others to act with confidence
5. Encouraging excellence in every action

There is much leadership joy in leading a team to win at something, but true love develops in the details of learning what works and why it works to produce the win. Understanding the details of any workplace process you are engaged in provides similar emotions. So, whatever you elected to endeavor to achieve, the quantity and quality of your commitment will determine the degree of your understanding for how and why it works and drive you to lead others toward a desired destination. This commitment to learning the details of the procedure will also provide for understanding problems with the process and how to correct those problems. The exceptional leader loves the work and develops a genuine interest in learning the intrinsic workings of the operation. To master the understanding of an operation is to love the process enough to want to know exactly how to lead others to love the process as well. Essentially, process patterns are the "operating manual" that describes which buttons to push or which play to run and when. And understanding what works for others, how to get others to follow, and why others want to follow you is understanding how to troubleshoot the specific details of exactly what is happening systematically when pushing the buttons or running a specific play fails to produce the intended outcome. Knowing "why" is critically important to your exceptional leadership. Knowing "why" others are willing to follow your leadership should be intrinsically vital to you.

Modeling What Success Looks Like

Great Leadership in Practice: Leadership is not a position of power and privilege; rather, it is a degree of respect for the position and level of responsibility to the organization. Leaders have

PRINCIPLE EIGHT: LEADERSHIP

many responsibilities, but the dominant responsibility is to model what success looks like in the performance of work. Your work is the vocation God has given you to do while here. Your work is who, what, and why you are. Only you can do the work God has given you to do. No one else but you can touch it or do it. Your work is your grind, and remember, you cannot cheat the grind. As the leader, I had to model what success looked like, on and off the job. I had to model great work ethics and habits. I had to model great performance. I had to model a great attitude, as attitude determines altitude. I had to play hard if I expected my teammates to play hard. I had to practice hard if I expected anyone else to practice hard. My job is not to tell anyone how to do their job. My job as a leader is to show my teammates what success looks like. It is up to them to do their work. I can only do my part. I lead by example. My teammates must decide if they want to follow. Modeling exceptionalism and high performance is the greatest responsibility of leadership.

One question I ask all leaders is, "Would you follow your leadership?" The question causes leaders to consider what exactly they are modeling that encourages others to want to follow them. A leader must model what they desire others around them to become, and success should be the model. If a leader expects employees to dress professionally, they must dress professionally themselves. If a leader encourages their staff to seek a work–life balance, they must show their team what a work–life balance looks like. As a leader in many organizations, I made it a practice to never ask employees to do anything I was not willing to do or did not know how to do. By knowing how, I was always able to model how I wanted success to look like. You cannot model something that you cannot do yourself.

First Exercise: List five things you believe you and every leader should model in the workplace that will lead the way to success.

Modeling what success looks like is the cornerstone of leading the way and is precisely the foundation that you build your leadership upon. A business, organization, or team must have a leader that everyone wants to follow. You are not a leader if you look around and no one is following you. There must be something about you that causes others to want to emulate some aspect of your being. Otherwise, there is no championship in your future. People generally want to follow successful people. If a business sets a goal of generating one million dollars in revenue for the year selling widgets, the leader must be able to model exactly what that looks like. How the leader dresses for work, the hours the leader works, and the leader's commitment to the operations are all looks of success the staff must desire to emulate. If the leader is never at work, dresses unprofessionally, and shows no commitment or knowledge of how to produce widgets, then he or she is a poor example to the team and will inspire no one to excellence. The leader must know more than just how to make widgets. The business must know how to make widgets in the most cost-effective manner. The business must know how to identify and access the widget market. In reaching its goal of one million dollars in revenue for the year, the business must know what works in all facets of the widget business and why, if the business is to be successful. Without this broad perspective and equitable knowledge, the leader will be unprepared to lead the way to success, and the company will just be warehousing widgets. Likewise, in professional sports team environments, the leader must model the way. The leader establishes team rules and must follow the rules herself or himself if he or she expects the players to follow the rules as well.

PRINCIPLE EIGHT: LEADERSHIP

A Leadership Performance Perspective: Leaders lead people to great destinations. The journey should be adventurous, and any adventure involves a degree of uncertainty and sacrifice. Oftentimes, leading the way can feel risky because the great leaders are always a few steps ahead of everyone else and may be stepping into the unknown. There are four ways that exceptional leaders address the risk associated with the adventurous journey of leading others to greatness.

4 WAYS LEADERS MODEL SUCCESS

1. **Always show up prepared.** The job of a leader is to be a couple of steps ahead. Leaders must study the markets and the landscape, evaluate and understand the potential risks and challenges, and prepare their teams for the journey. But the leader must prepare himself or herself first. The leader must get prepared and stay prepared, so that they are always ready. *Proper Preparation Produces Peak Performance*, and the exceptional leader must model the 5 Ps.

2. **Sacrifice personal interest.** The job of the leader is not just to be the example but also to put the team before himself or herself. The journey can be tough and require everyone to sacrifice self-interests. The leaders must be willing to sacrifice more than all others. Leaders look for opportunities to lighten the load for others so that the team wins.

3. **Set the appropriate pace.** Leaders tend to run ahead of everyone. Many are in positions of leadership because of their demonstrated ability to forge ahead with great speed. Leaders must realize that the pace they set must be one that others can maintain. One must never outrun their team. Leaders are energized by the challenge and opportunity to be successful. They are extremely eager to get to

their destination. But they must slow down and set a pace that the rest of their team can keep up with or risk losing the team and finding only themselves at the top. The top can be a lonely place if you are the only one standing there. So, set the appropriate pace, and others will match your speed. When I served onboard the USS Enterprise, it was known that the huge aircraft carrier was faster than the cruisers and other ships that escorted the aircraft carrier. Occasionally, and when circumstances allowed, captains of the escort ships would challenge our captain to a race in the middle of the Indian Ocean. While the USS Enterprise was the slowest to reach top speed, once it did reach top speed, the race was not even close. The USS Enterprise and her escorts were battleships built for war. While the Enterprise was faster than her escorts, she had to set a pace during normal operations for all other ships. She had to set a pace that all could keep up with, for what is an aircraft carrier in the middle of the ocean without her escorts? Leaders must ask themselves the same question: Who am I if I am in the middle of the ocean all alone because I have outpaced my entire team?

4. **Celebrate others' success.** Leaders must be the head cheerleader and must celebrate the success of each staff member. Celebrating others encourages everyone to do their best. When the leader is seen celebrating the success of others, the act becomes contagious and creates a culture of collaboration, team building, and innovation. Celebrating success is a great means of reminding your team of the goal to win. By modeling a celebratory atmosphere, the operational vision is kept consistently in front of the team and informs and guides them to the desired destination.

PRINCIPLE EIGHT: LEADERSHIP

Leaders must understand the inner workings of human dynamics that causes one to desire to follow another. No one is interested in following a loser. Winners are the ones who look back and see large crowds following. Do you remember the massive crowd that engulfed Tiger Woods when he was walking to the greens on the 18th hole on his way to ending a five-year drought by winning the 2018 Tour Championship? People eagerly follow winners! A leader must demonstrate the role of leadership in a manner that makes their leadership attractive. Woods always made it attractive. Someone must be attracted enough to your leadership success to want to follow. Without a follower, one cannot be a leader. Leading the way, modeling what success looks like, and inspiring a common destination is the responsibility of great leadership.

Inspiring a Common Destination

"If you want to build a ship, do not drum up the people to gather wood, divide the work, and give orders. Instead, teach every one of them to yearn for the vast and endless sea."
—*Antoine De Saint-Exupery*

Inspiring a common destination is key to experiencing greater leadership success, improving employee engagement, and increasing the organization's overall financial performance and operational efficiency. *A common destination can be defined as an end goal or objective that a leader and their team establish and work towards together.* People are always interested in a great adventure. A great leader will always inspire their team to work toward a common destination that everyone involved is excited about. Inspiring a common destination helps employees see a deeper meaning in their daily work instead of feeling as if they are performing tedious routine tasks that don't contribute to any particular organizational goal or vision. Inspiring a common destination begins with listening to your team rather than dictating their every action. Take time to actively listen to those around you to determine what aspires them to be their best. Know what their goals and aspirations are. Know what they hope for and envision in their lives, both at work and in their personal lives. How do they see themselves in the organization's future? While people go to work to obtain a paycheck, they require much more than the check to remain excited about the job. They must be excited about the direction the company is moving in. The exceptional leader labors to know what compels the team members to continue working in the organization. Understanding the motivation of your staff leads to getting everyone focused on the common destination. Once you have solicited your employees to share their interests, share with them the possibilities you envision. Paint as clear of a picture as you can about your vision for the organization. This will cause your staff to be more excited about winning the championship.

Exercise: List five things a leader can do to inspire a common destination.

4 TIPS TO INSPIRE A COMMON DESTINATION
1. Make thinking about the past and present success of the organization a common leadership activity and consider how the past and present inform the future you intend to create for your organization. Be visionary.
2. Solicit the ideas, aspirations, goals, and vision from others for what the future looks like for them and consider how

the interests of others align with the greater organizational goals and vision. Be inclusive.
3. Demonstrate to staff how a common destination for the team can help them achieve success, win championships, and meet their long-term goals. Be inspiring.
4. Routinely re-evaluate your goals, vision, and aspirations and determine if others are excited about the future of the organization and their roles in the process. Be innovative.

To fully understand just how well you are inspiring a common destination, it's very important for a leader to periodically stop and look backward and reflect upon who is following and why are they following. This reflection should drive an action that leads the team effectively toward your goals. A leader should maintain a series of questions to ask themselves and their team to insure the inspiration of a common destination.

QUESTIONS TO ASK YOURSELF AS YOU INSPIRE A COMMON DESTINATION

- What is the current common destination?
- Are others inspired to work toward our common destination?
- Where do I see the organization in 10 years?
- Where do I see myself in 10 years?
- What are the three highest priorities for the organization?
- Am I doing a great job of sharing my vision?
- Am I doing a great job of asking others their goals?
- What do I see in my future and the future of the organization?

Inspiring a common destination requires leaders to be creative, innovative, and staunch visionaries who engage others in creating an adventurous future. Remember, humans love a great adventure. Leaders should make it a common practice to bring their teams along for the adventure, soliciting their ideas, goals, and visions and defining the common destination the entire team desires to journey toward.

Challenging Others to Maximize Performance

Inevitably, and occasionally, all leaderships and organizations hit bumps on the path to success. Those bumps interrupt the efficient or effective paths of an otherwise good process or team environment. The largest bump that impedes the path to success is the bump of being "good enough." The natural enemy to "best" is "good enough." Poor performance is typically the result of a series of unplanned events that can lead to mediocrity and everyone being satisfied with just being good enough. This is why the exceptional leader must be prepared to challenge "good enough." Knowing what makes the workplace process work and knowing why it works proves critical to a leader's ability to right what has gone wrong in the process. If the path of high performance and great success is interrupted by "good enough" or great relationships among team members are disenfranchised by dishonesty and mistrust, what works and why it does work to restore excellence or rebuild honesty and trust will become the foundation for increasing job performance or rebuilding the relationships. Without such knowledge of how to incite the workforce to abandon the valley of mediocre performance and chase excellence, the organization will surely never know great success.

A Leadership Development Perspective: If you want teammates, employees, and coworkers who are engaged and energized about

PRINCIPLE EIGHT: LEADERSHIP

performing at their best, they must understand how their actions align with the ideas, goals, and vision of the organization. If the goal is to win a Superbowl, then everyone must realize that is the goal and then work to perform at the necessary level, and the leader must be prepared to challenge "good enough" and drive everyone to be their best. Have you ever listened to someone talk about winning a championship and get so drawn in by the story that you felt compelled to go do more than you've ever done to increase your own performance? Storytelling is a great tool for driving positive change and challenging your team to achieve amazing accomplishments. Teams win championships when everyone on the team comes together, inspired by a common destination, and are challenged to do their best for a cause greater than themselves. Hearing someone talk about how they won a championship can inspire you to do your best. Think about how you talk to your team. Are you already challenging them to do their best with your leadership actions? Are you demonstrating your "best" and challenging their "good enough?" Exceptional leadership begins with sharing that exciting adventure that leads to an amazing destination. The visionary leader shares his or her vision of where he or she sees the organization or team a year or two later. Then the leader describes what is needed from every single person on the team to make that vision of success a reality. Coach Tomlin, who led the Steelers to a Superbowl his second year as head coach, said: "Every day is a great opportunity." To challenge your team, be excited and detailed about short- and long-term goals and how each person's performance is critical for the team's success, and convince them that there is great opportunity in every day. When you project a clear picture of what the future looks like, you allow the team to imagine what they need to accomplish. You are challenging "good enough" when you do so. This is how teams win championships. This is how you can drive your organization to unprecedented levels of success. This is how coach Tomlin became the youngest coach to win a Superbowl in 2009.

An exceptional leader must be a visionary, someone who can see beyond what is visible and imagine what is possible. A leader must share that vision in a clear and attractive manner. Where the organization is going, the common destination, must be so appealing that it drives every employee to abandon the notion of "good enough" to work tirelessly to become their "best." Employees must be shown the future and then challenged to pursue the vision with excitement and expectation. Essentially, the leader must show his or her employees why they should care to be their best. As a leader, it is your responsibility to always ask what is next and drive others to improve their performance year after year. You have attracted the top talent; now, share your vision with those who can help you bring it to reality. You do not have to be an expert or a genius to encourage people to follow your lead and embrace your vision. You just need to be truly passionate about what you are doing and drive others to be their absolute best. Care enough to share personal stories; they work best. Be positive and be the example, even when there are bumps in the road. Don't forget to celebrate every success and be mindful, setting time aside to reflect and plan before you act. And, above all, always remember to involve others in developing your vision. When employees are intrinsically connected to the vision, they automatically show up with the mindset of being their absolute best.

Empowering Others to Act with Confidence

Being empowered is the difference between having opportunity in your circumstances and having power over your

PRINCIPLE EIGHT: LEADERSHIP

circumstances. An exceptional leader ensures their staff has power over their circumstances, not simply opportunity. Most Americans above the age of 18 have learned to drive a motor vehicle of some sort. Being able to drive a vehicle is having the power to transport yourself and not having to rely on others for a ride. Leaders enable their team to drive, not simply go along for the ride. Teaching someone to drive an automobile is an excellent example of empowering others to act. When we teach our teenage children how to drive the family car, we make them less dependent on us, and we give them control over their circumstances. We also help them develop a sense of responsibility that only comes with the power of control. When my father taught me how to drive his old 1968 Ford Galaxy 500, he just taught me the very basics of driving. He taught me how to start the engine with the automobile in park and how to place my foot on the brake pedal when I move the transmission from park into reverse or drive. He taught me to slowly push down on the gas pedal initially and how to stay on my side of the road when driving. He also taught me how to slow down and signal before turning. I slowly learned the basics of driving, and I was eventually licensed to drive after passing my driver's test. The basic knowledge of how to drive empowered me in certain circumstances to drive myself from place to place without having to rely on someone else. Driving provided me with greater independence as a teenager. That basic knowledge gave me the opportunity in my circumstances to develop greater responsibility for my own well-being. Allowing others to develop greater responsibility for their own well-being is the essence of leadership.

My father was a master automobile mechanic. He had the ability to completely dismantle an automobile engine and reassemble the engine to perfect operating condition. As a result of having a master automobile mechanic as a father, I learned a tremendous amount about how an automobile operated and why some mechanical parts operated as they did. Because of my father's abilities, I received more than just basic knowledge of automobiles. As fate, circumstance, and statistics would have it, I was approximately 100 miles from home one late evening driving from college in my mother's old Oldsmobile; these cars are not even manufactured anymore. Suddenly, the lights started to get dimmer and dimmer as I was driving. I finally had to pull off the freeway due to having insufficient lighting from the car's headlights to continue. But because I had learned so much about vehicles from a master automobile mechanic, I knew that the problem was more than likely caused by the alternator not working properly. Sure enough, when I checked, I found a loose alternator wire and tightened it. And knowing that a bad alternator also results in the battery being drained, I summoned another motorist to jump start my car battery to give the vehicle the start it needed. Once the vehicle started, the alternator was able to perform its function to run the vehicle and recharge the battery. I eventually made it home safely. Understanding how the alternator worked and why empowered me to act on my own behalf and gave me control over my circumstance. Instead of being stranded 100 miles from home, I was able to right what was wrong with the vehicle and continue my journey. This identifies the ultimate purpose of why leaders should empower others. A leader cannot always be there, just as we cannot always be there for our children. Understanding the intricate operations in the workplace allows you to provide the necessary training and development. When employees are properly trained, they are given power over their circumstances.

When things go wrong and the boss is not around, they are empowered to make corrections and keep the operations on track so that the team can continue the journey to success. Having advanced knowledge of how automobiles operate, and not just the basics, provided me with control over my circumstances. I was able to make the necessary mechanical adjustments to my vehicle so that I could continue on and successfully make it home. Without the knowledge of how an automobile worked, my routine process pattern of traveling between home and college would have been seriously interrupted. I had traveled that I-75 freeway corridor in Tennessee that traversed between my hometown of Bakewell and my college town of Knoxville often. I knew the directions for a successful route home. That pattern and route was always successful until that one fateful night when things did not go as planned. As a leader, you must empower your staff, because as fate, circumstance, and statistics will surely prove, there will be stalls in operations. Operations experience unplanned and unexpected anomalies at the most inopportune times. The exceptional leader ensures that his or her team is always empowered to act so that it is never stranded 100 miles from their destination.

Exercise: List five things a leader can do to empower others to act.

Before you embark upon a successful journey in an automobile, you must know a few things about your vehicle. Does the car have a good set of tires? Are the tires properly inflated, balanced, and of good thread depth? If the tires are not properly inflated, not balanced, or lack good tread depth, this would present certain risks to completing the path you plan to travel safely. Does the car have enough gas in the tank to complete the trip? A leader must ask similar questions in the workplace. Are you prepared for challenges in your processes? Are you ready to adapt to changes? Have you gained the advanced knowledge required to troubleshoot the problems that materialize in your process patterns? Whatever your personal or professional situation may be, make sure you are completely prepared for the journey you have chosen to embark upon. If you have failed to prepare in any manner, you are subject to having your journey interrupted because of your poor preparation, and a major part of any preparation is possessing advanced knowledge of systems and processes involved in your endeavor so that you understand how to react to adversity along the way. If you are prepared, then you must prepare your team as well. A team cannot win an NBA title if the coach is the only person prepared. A coach must empower their team to win. A leader must empower their team to succeed in the workplace. Winning championships requires advanced knowledge, not just the basics. Advanced knowledge in professional disciplines and team building assist in keeping you on track when unplanned situations arise. Remember, once you have established your path to success, there are no short cuts to this success, only distractions, interruptions, and delays. Knowing how to properly deal with those unplanned events will determine the very quality of the journey. Have you empowered others to act?

"You can eliminate mistakes by developing advanced knowledge. Focusing on training and development provides an atmosphere of confidence in your work and promotes a foundation for growth and high performance. You cannot get better at something until you understand what you are

doing, down to the most miniscule of details. Without understanding this, success is only a matter of luck, and failure is simply a matter of time."

—Ronald T. Hickey

Encouraging Excellence in Every Action

The Ukrainian Chernobyl reactor plant was a four-reactor nuclear reactor plant centrally located between what was then known as Belarus, Ukraine, and the Soviet Union of Russia. On April 25, 1986, prior to a routine shut down, the reactor crew at Chernobyl-4 began preparing for a test to determine how long the turbines would continue to spin and supply power following a loss of main electrical power supply. This test was being conducted even though these reactors were known to be very unstable at low power settings due to a flawed design. A series of interruptions in the test caused the reactor to be in this unstable low power condition for an extended period. Additionally, operator actions, including the disabling of protective automatic shutdown mechanisms, preceded the attempted test early on April 26, 1986. As flow of coolant water diminished, power output increased. When the operator moved to shut down the reactor from its unstable condition arising from previous errors, a peculiarity of the design caused a dramatic power surge. The fuel elements ruptured, and the resultant explosive force of steam lifted the cover plate off the reactor vessel, releasing radioactive fission products to the atmosphere. A second explosion threw out fragments of burning fuel and graphite from the core and allowed air to rush in, causing the graphite moderator to burst into flames. Approximately 50 deaths are attributed to this nuclear reactor accident. The Chernobyl nuclear reactor accident is a great reminder to the world and leaders in every global company or organization that we must encourage excellence in everything we do. Chernobyl was an accident that could have and should have been prevented. If the operators had been encouraged by a culture of excellence, they might not have disabled the automatic protection that would have shut down the reactor prior to any explosions, and this incident would never have happened, at least not on April 26, 1986. I was working as a nuclear engineer in the United States Navy at the time of this incident. After learning of what the initial reports offered as the cause, I took a serious look at our nuclear operations onboard the USS Enterprise and re-evaluated all our processes. I assembled my team and immediately took actions to encourage excellence in everything we did in the nuclear reactor plants onboard the Enterprise.

The Chernobyl nuclear power plant operators disabled the automatic computer control to override a protection feature during a testing operation and then did not know how to manually operate the reactor systems when the need arose. Reports suggest that the operators were poorly trained and had only a basic understanding of nuclear theory and an even less understanding of the particular design of the Chernobyl reactors. There was absolutely no culture of excellence embedded in any of their processes. I am aware that nuclear theory can be a challenge to understand, but I believe this incident clearly makes the case for how important it is to fully understand what you are engaged in. I understand that few businesses are as dangerous and complicated as controlling nuclear fission. But we do go to retail stores and routinely find shelves not properly stocked. Companies can melt down in a variety of manners when excellence is not the standard. You have surely heard

PRINCIPLE EIGHT: LEADERSHIP

someone say, "He knows just enough to be dangerous." Having only basic knowledge can get you into trouble, whether you are stocking shelves at Walmart or operating a nuclear reactor or leading a school district. Advanced knowledge keeps you out of trouble. Not being properly trained causes simple mistakes that could result in catastrophic incidents and major damages, or worse, unfortunate deaths due to radiation fallout. So, it is not enough for leaders to empower their staff, but the exceptional leader encourages excellence in everything his or her team does. When excellence describes the culture, the leader is leading the way. The next time you frequent your favorite retail establishment, your ability or inability to find every item on your shopping list is a clear reflection of leadership within the store and organization. Your own leadership reflects in a similar manner. What are your customers saying about you? What does your staff say about you and your leadership.

Exercise: List five things a leader can do to create a culture of excellence in the workplace.

I recall when I was employed with a company that manufactured rocket casings. One evening, an operator was overseeing the production of the casing. A large rotating device that assisted in the manufacturing process experienced some binding in the bearings. As a result, the bearings overheated. When the operator sensed the overheating condition, he attempted to cool the bearings by applying a wet rag to the bearing housing. The rag he applied happened to be soaked with a liquid chemical mixture with a low flashpoint. The flammable chemical and cloth material, combined with the heat from the bearings, resulted in a fire. The fire caused enough damage to the rocket casing that resulted in the casing being discarded. Essentially, the rocket casing was destroyed by the fire that was caused by the operator exposing the overheated bearings to a flammable liquid. The discarded casing was a $500,000 loss for the company. Driving a culture of excellence into every process can help avoid making costly mistakes and save lives. In this case, the operator knew very little about his operations. Until the incident, the company had only been lucky with this "low-knowledge" employee working with a "good enough" mindset. Training and development were lacking, and there was no culture of excellence. Failure was simply a matter of time.

I fear that we are building organizations on a foundation of mediocrity in America. Far too many Americans have this hotel culture mentality of expecting convenience over challenges; we want room service. We are living in a time where we can pull up an app on our mobile devices and have McDonalds delivered within 30 minutes. Creating this culture of excellence in everything we do in the workplace is even more critical than ever before. Our organizational successes tend to exist in the margins of our programs instead of in the great body of our work. Why is excellence in the workplace the exception and not the rule? The culture of excellence starts with education and the ability to attract top talent. Don't discount the value of knowledge. There is premium on top talent. A high-performing employee produces 10 times the work of the average employee. Let excellence be a common destination your organization journeys toward. We know what works, but we fail to act. Why are we settling down in this valley of mediocrity and low performance in this country? I have yet to find a good answer. Instead, I find passivity. Exceptional leadership is not passive. Exceptional leadership is taking a serious look at every aspect

PRINCIPLE EIGHT: LEADERSHIP

of your organization and driving a culture of excellence down to the quantum level in all operations. America is starving for truly smart people who truly understand what works in the workplace and who are ready to lead the way. Are you that truly smart leader who is ready to lead the way to the destination of excellence? The success of our lives and our organizations depends on our ability to bring resolve to this very pressing crisis of low performance and mediocre outcomes. Let us all commit to encouraging excellence in everything we do! This is the primary responsibility of exceptional leadership.

PRINCIPLE NINE

Expectations

Expectations: The Exceptional leader has high expectations.

"You will be successful when you expect to be successful; because believe it or not, you are always right about yourself. If you say you can, you can. If you say you can't, you can't."
—Ronald T. Hickey

The reason so many leaders, and people in general, fail to experience their full potential is because success and reaching their full potential are not the expectation. Humans tend to get to a place in life where good is good enough. When one doesn't truly believe they have the talents and abilities to achieve the things they say they want to achieve, this lack of self-confidence causes them not to expect much out of themselves. When one tells themselves they can't, it becomes a self-fulfilling prophesy. If one expects they can't, they can't. If one expects they can, they can. If a leader believes and expects that they will be exceptional, they will be exceptional. Often, our own disbelief in our capacity to accomplish a task prevents us from being successful. While someone outside and beyond us may plant the idea in our minds that we cannot succeed at something, our own willingness to accept and believe the same is the true reason many of us continue to live a life of mediocrity. Simply stated, our inability to trust in ourselves, our abilities, our talents, and our

PRINCIPLE NINE: EXPECTATIONS

knowledge is precisely why we experience low expectations and, thus, low achievements in our lives. Each of us can significantly change our conditions for the better simply by believing we can do the things we say we want to do and expect success. Decide today that your life is going to be everything you wish your life to be and believe with all your heart and soul that you have all the abilities necessary to bring your desired life into full fruition. Say you can, and you will, and you will immediately start to grow toward the light of success. Know that if you expect you can, you can. So, on this spot, on this day, expect that you can be a great leader. Greatness is what greatness does, and one must first expect greatness. If you don't know how to achieve greatness, learn what it takes. If you don't have what it takes to be great, go get what it takes. From this day forth, make your leadership count and do not falter in your expectations to fulfill your destiny. Believe with all that you are that God has given you all that you need to become the greatest leader you can be. Believe in yourself and the abilities bestowed upon your being and expect the success you desire. Refuse, wholeheartedly, to follow some false destiny outlined in some mystical imaginative world. Understand what you are capable of, stay in your leadership lane, and create your own unique style of leading others. Trust in your own abilities and be the best version of you!

A leader's resolve to leave deep footprints on the path they travel is their best asset. Without such drive and motivation, a leader suffers a separate defeat each day. While an occasional defeat is unavoidable, let it not be from loss of will, low expectations, or lack of resolve but because you have nothing left to give and your time is over. Every leader has the ability to do something on a grand scale. Expectation determines just how grand it will be. Exceptional leaders understand that life is a process in which one collects along the adventurous journey all that is required to achieve at the highest level. Exceptional leaders do not give up their resolve to imprint upon this earth their true gifts of greatness. When others say great leaders can do no more, they keep moving and prove otherwise. Exceptional leaders achieve to the exact degree they expect to achieve. As long as you can keep going, use your imagination to cope with the travails of leadership, for leading other humans is the most challenging undertaking of this human endeavor. Great leaders are never burdened beyond what they can accomplish, no matter how heavy the burden may seem at times. God's weight is never meant to break you but to shape you. Overcome your obstacles and realize what you envision and expect to achieve what you imagine. If you lack the education to move up in your organization, go back to school and gain the necessary education. If you know you don't have the funds to start a business you have always dreamed of owning and operating, get a second job or third job to save the money. If something is standing in the way of your achievement, trust in your abilities to go around, under, over, or through the obstacle. If your spouse, friend, coworker, or anyone is telling you that you cannot do something and you know that you can, do not listen and do what you know you are capable of. Do not surround yourself with people who are rooting for you to lose. Those who really want you to win will also help you do the digging.

I recall years ago when I sat across the table from an education counselor who told me I would not make it through the Naval Nuclear Power School in Orlando, Florida. At the time, when I was enrolled in the Navy's Nuclear Power School, the school was ranked #2, only to MIT, in the country

PRINCIPLE NINE: EXPECTATIONS

based on the attrition rate of students. I understood that the school would be my greatest academic challenge, but I knew and trusted my abilities. Because I knew I was handsomely adorned with intellectual capacity, I expected to be successful in any academic setting. This counselor knew nothing of me; he definitely knew nothing of my internal drive and belief in my own abilities. All he knew of me was contained in the academic record sitting in front of him in a manila folder. My academic record only conveyed that I was a highly intelligent person with no known academic limits. I rejected the words of the counselor and graduated from the school in the highest percentile. A few years later, while serving on board the aircraft carrier, the USS Enterprise, I was in charge of all electrical plant operations for four nuclear reactor plants. A year after that, I oversaw all electrical systems training for a 500-personnel reactor department. But the counselor had told me I was not going to make it through the Nuclear Power school. I had the final say in this matter. I trusted in my knowledge, talents, and academic abilities. I said I could, and I did. I expected I would be successful, and I was successful. *Greatness Is What Greatness Does.*

In no way am I suggesting that your leadership will not know unexpected failure and moments of low performance. Life is not perfect, and things do not always work out the way we desire. Life is very challenging at times, and no one wins every single time. Accept that fact, but do not allow setbacks to cause you to doubt yourself or your leadership. The nature of human existence ensures that we will experience the bitterness of life, but the power of trusting in our own abilities will guarantee that such sourness is short lived. Know that you will stumble in life and leadership, but trust that you will always have the ability to get back up on your feet and complete the adventurous journey that leads to greatness. Know that you will come up short in the race on one day but capture the gold medal in the next competition. Life is a dualistic existence. We fail and succeed in life. We rise and fall. We live and die. At times, we must fail so we can succeed, fall so we can rise, or even die so we can live. Nothing in life is so static that it cannot evolve, and there is nothing in life so dynamic that it can't be brought down. How we handle the peaks and valleys of life and leadership ultimately determines the heights of our overall travel. The worst thing you can do is get down on yourself and start wasting precious time buffering the facts of life with fairy tales and illogical explanations. I have learned that failures, defeats, setbacks, and sorrow all have intrinsic lessons that ultimately provide me with some invaluable knowledge and understanding that will be valuable in the future and guide my expectations and, ultimately, my success. Experiencing certain situations is the only way of gaining a particular knowledge at times. God causes us to suffer defeat today so that we can be triumphant tomorrow. Through the suffering, we must believe and trust that we are going to be better on the other end. Even when we fail, we must believe that if we try again, we can fail better. If we are willing to fail better, then we can map the path to success. Imagine the suffering that Tony Dungy and his family were required to endure with the loss of his oldest child. Tony Dungy emerged from that situation believing and trusting more in God, his family, his team, and his abilities. As a result, the following year he was the first African American head football coach in the NFL to lead his team to a Super Bowl championship. Tony's setback was a setup for greatness. *Greatness Is What Greatness Does.*

PRINCIPLE NINE: EXPECTATIONS

"In life, all one ever needs is an opportunity to make his or her life count. When you get the opportunity to be your best, do your part and be great at it."
—Dr. Ollie R. Mack

I have asked myself if I could suffer as Tony Dungy and his family were required to suffer and emerge from such tragedy continuing to trust life, myself, and my abilities. I am sure many of you have wondered about such. As I stated earlier, you are capable of bearing your cross, even though you may not think so at the time of burden. I imagine that in spite of the catastrophe, Tony Dungy still saw the opportunity in his circumstance for greatness. If you lose or have lost your job, trust that your abilities will ensure you will find a better job. If your company is in trouble, trust that you have the knowledge to right all that is going wrong and make your company stronger. Despite the adversity, expectations rule the day. Adversity aids the tempering process of life and leadership. Always be able to see the opportunity in your circumstances and make everything count. Just as steal is subjected to extreme heat and cold temperatures in the tempering process to make the steal almost unbreakable, adversity is the heat that tempers your leadership and makes you a stronger and more durable leader. The tempering of your leadership is necessary for you to achieve high levels of sustainable achievements. Despite the travails of your leadership, do your part and be great anyway.

Ray Kroc, who started McDonald's Fast Foods, was a milkshake machine salesman until he joined the McDonald brothers, who operated a one-restaurant fast food hamburger business in Southern California. Mr. Kroc eventually purchased the restaurant from the McDonald's brothers in 1961 and franchised the business into what McDonald's is today, a global fast food chain of restaurants. Ray Kroc died in 1984 with a reported net worth of $600 million at his death. He was also the owner of the San Diego Padres from 1974 until his death. Imagine all that Ray Kroc had to suffer through. Tempering is not intended to weaken you but to strengthen you with unyielding confidence and wisdom that your God-given talents and developed abilities will deliver the life you desire if only you trust, believe, and expect big things out of yourself. With such trust and expectations, you must fulfill everything you want in life and leadership. Your life is a creation that evolves as you desire, expect, and believe you will. Trust that you can, and you will. Give up your doubtful notions, and in so doing, you will finally emerge completely in your destiny for greatness. Until that moment of grandiosity, create the successful pathways of your leadership with confidence, passion, purpose, expectation, and determination.

Exercise: List five things you expect to achieve as an exceptional leader.

> *"I've spent most of my life walking under that hovering cloud, self-doubt, whose acid raindrops blurred my vision and burned holes in my heart. Once I learned to use the umbrella of confidence, the skies cleared up for me and the sunshine called joy became my faithful companion."*
> —Astrid Alauda

After my military career came to an end in 1992, I went to work for a global industrial metals company. I was hired as a journeyman electrician in one of the company's many industrial

PRINCIPLE NINE: EXPECTATIONS

manufacturing plants. This particular plant was located in the California Bay Area. After about six months on the job, my supervisor resigned for a better opportunity with another company. The plant was in the middle of an expansion project to provide for an increase in production capacity. Part of the expansion project included 150 yards of additional conveyance belts controlled by a programmable limit controller (PLC) that included computer-operated sensors, motors, and other electrical peripherals. The entire project had been designed by engineers at the company's headquarters back East. My supervisor, who had just resigned, was the one who usually did all the programming of the PLCs in the plant. PLCs were a new industry device in the early 1990s, and I knew very little about them since the Navy, where I had been the past 8 years, had not advanced at the same rate as technology. But I knew the basics and learned all I could about PLCs every opportunity I had. While I had only been there six months, I knew more about the new technology than the other electricians who had been working at the plant for years but had no interest in learning the new technology. So, when my supervisor walked out the door, the big expansion project was put on hold. No one at the plant could program the PLCs, and corporate could not spare an engineer to respond to the Bay Area for the time required to write the ladder logic program that was required to make the system operate and then test the system for proper operations. So, the thousands of dollars' worth of new equipment just sat idle. I knew I understood the basics of writing ladder logic, and I knew I had the ability to review the designs for the expansion project and determine how everything was intended to operate. Thus, I took the initiative to take a few manuals home. I learned, to the advanced level, all there was to know about PLCs and writing ladder logic for PLC programs. After two weeks of reading manuals, I expected to make the system work as intended because I had confidence in my abilities. I would spend my lunch and work breaks for the next five to six weeks working on finishing the expansion project. I tested all the electrical motors, sensors, counters, interlocks, and all other electrical and mechanical devices for proper operations. Before my employment with Reynolds Metals, I was leading the electrical plant operations of nuclear power plants in the Navy. I expected that writing ladder logic would be within my capabilities if I could operate nuclear reactors. I ran the conveyor system to ensure the computer program I had written controlled the entire operation per plans. No one at the plant was aware of what I was doing on my own time. I completely developed the ladder logic for the PLC for the 150 yards of conveyance. I wrote the ladder logic to operate the system based on how the engineering designs suggested everything should work. I recall the night I loaded the ladder logic into the main PLC module for the first time during my shift lunch break. On my laptop, I initiated a run signal for the program to operate the large conveyance system, and like magic, everything operated as I expected it would. I had to make some minor adjustments in the ladder logic and adjust the positions of some sensors associated with the conveyor system. But everything worked. Before I realized it, I had an audience. Everyone on the night crew was wondering what all this new equipment operating was and how it was going to make things better. In about an hour, the plant manager had returned to the plant. He had been called by another employee and told what I was doing. He demanded that I demonstrate all that I had done. Once he was absolutely sure everything was operating as required, he finally shook my hand

PRINCIPLE NINE: EXPECTATIONS

and told me to meet him in his office the next morning at 10:00 AM. When I arrived for the meeting, he offered me the supervisor's position that was still vacant. I trusted my abilities and was confident that I could learn what I needed to know to make the new conveyance project a success. In less than seven months on the job, I was promoted over employees who had worked in the plant for more than 25 years. I expected that I could, and I did. As a result, I became the new supervisor of the electrical division. Promotions are the ultimate pay off for trusting in your own knowledge and expecting to be successful. *Greatness Is What Greatness Does.*

Expectation is not some blind attribute built on a hope creed. Expectation comes from trusting in your own ability, and it is intended to lead to self-sufficiency and self-assuredness. Remember from the previous principle that exceptional leaders must lead the way, and we lead the way with confidence in our abilities. No one else assisted me in the conveyance project. As a result of my self-sufficiency and self-assuredness, the plant I worked in did not have to rely on headquarters for engineering services, so the plant was self-sufficient as a result. The new conveyor system doubled the plant's production capacity. Whatever one needs in life, one should be able to impact one's own well-being. Being able to help yourself does not mean you will always have or know what you need at any given moment. Just like in the conveyance example above, sometimes you must delay moving forward until you have taken the time to understand your limits and have gone out and gained the knowledge necessary to satisfy the challenges associated with situations you find yourself in. But you must trust you that have the ability to do such. Whether one is stranded on the highway 100 miles from home or dealing with poor performance in the workplace or dealing with a domestic project requiring the understanding of municipal codes and civil procedures, one should be able to cope with aplomb and ease. But you must first expect to do so.

A Leadership Performance Prospective: *Mike Tomlin became the second African American to lead a National Football League franchise to a Super Bowl championship on February 1, 2009. He accomplished this outstanding feat at the age of 36 and during his second season as the head coach of the Pittsburg Steelers. When asked by a sports reporter referencing his youthfulness and short tenure as head coach if he ever doubted his ability and experience to lead the franchise to their record sixth Super Bowl championship, Mike Tomlin replied that he never doubted his abilities. He affirmed that the Rooney family, the owners of the Pittsburg Steelers, knows the business of football. Mike Tomlin stated that if the Rooney's had enough confidence in him to give him the job, then he knew he had all the necessary tools for being successful. Mike Tomlin told himself that he could win a Super Bowl championship as the head coach of the Pittsburg Steelers; He expected to win a Super Bowl, and he did just that in only two years.*

While being very successful comes with a great deal of self-sufficiency and confidence, being self-sufficient and confident can drive your expectations in such a manner that it causes isolation. I have observed leaders attempt to do everything themselves. I have attempted to do everything myself, at times, for the sake of guaranteeing things get done correctly. While I am successful in those moments, I find myself feeling isolated on islands of success. What have we accomplished if we are the only person grinding to success on our team? It is not enough to simply expect success of yourself; you must drive the same expectation into the mindset of everyone on your team

PRINCIPLE NINE: EXPECTATIONS

if winning is the goal, if increasing revenue is the goal, and if meeting the expectations of shareholders is the goal. A leader does not succeed in isolation. You cannot expect to do everything yourself and block everyone else out of the process. This is a very important point to understand. When the Emperor of China closed the borders, the country was self-sufficient enough to enjoy the isolation. The entire nation withdrew into a magical contentment. But eventually, an inbred society developed. Stagnation and decay set in. An identical issue can arise in a leader who believes they are so self-sufficient that they fail to engage the human endeavor fully and involve others. As a leader, you will implode from the sheer weight of your own decadence and stagnation, or you will explode once the outside world confronts you with something you cannot handle alone. Just as China began to flourish and experience the greatness of life once it reopened its borders to the outside world, leaders must remain open to the influences, stimuli, and information of others if they are to experience the possibilities of greatness. Leadership cannot be lived in a vacuum, at least not an exceptional leadership. The grandiosity of leadership cannot be realized by only wandering about the margins of this human episode. The abundance of leadership is nebulous in nature, and every situation, condition, and time has the potential for providing explosive potential to push you more and more in the direction of that common destination. Expect success as you traverse the abyss of organizational operations as you follow the intuitions of your heart and take each step with your team working as hard as you with the confidence that you are where you are as a result of the daily grind that you and your team muster together. Step out of the margins and onto the full pages of your leadership with intrepidness and determination and a

GREATNESS IS WHAT GREATNESS DOES

well-trained, highly motivated, and greatness-expecting team. Trust in you! And trust in your team! Leaders who trust in their own abilities and trust in the abilities of their people rule their environment without bounds, and they win championships.

> *"Every day, we slaughter our finest impulses. That is why we get a heartache when we read those lines written by the hand of a master and recognize them as our own, as the tender shoots which we stifled because we lacked the faith to believe in our own powers, our own criterion of truth and beauty. Every man, when he gets quiet, when he becomes desperately honest with himself, is capable of uttering profound truths. We all derive from the same source. There is no mystery about the origin of things. We are all part of creation, all kings, all poets, all musicians; we have only to open up to discover what is already there."*
>
> —Henry Miller, *Sexus*

You may be capable of great things, but you must open up and discover what is already within you. True expectation is internal. You may only see little things when you look at yourself. You may be in the infancy of your leadership. You may not have experienced a major victory yet. You may still be in the building process with your team. You may not be exactly where you want to be. Do not suppress those little things because life consists overwhelmingly of small things. Big things seldom come along. You should embrace the small things about your leadership as well as the big things. The big and the small have made you who you are. Big things do not occur until a lot of little things have come together on behalf of some great accomplishment. A big book is but an orderly collection of a volume of small words

PRINCIPLE NINE: EXPECTATIONS

combined in such a manner that they convey a literary context. Your big life is but a summation of all the small daily things you have accomplished. Remember, you crawled before you walked. You mumbled small words before you uttered a complete sentence. The small things we complete give rise to our beliefs that we are capable of something larger. We may all desire vehemently to experience grand and lasting achievements, to invent a new process or product that makes our company billions of dollars, or to be the one who saves the failing organization, but life seldom affords us the opportunities to make billions, become heroes, or accomplish great achievements. But we all have the ability to be great at the small things that dominate our lives and our leadership. We can be great at small daily activities and interactions that make us great coworkers and contributors on the team. We can be great at listening to our friends, fishing with our grandfather, shopping with our mother, or cooking with our family. The grandiosity of life emerges from our unwavering ability to excel at these small things. If a child does not master the science of math or the art of English, they cannot become a great scientist or famous orator one day. If you want to be a highly successful leader, give much attention to mastering the small things. If you don't master the small steps of leadership, you will not develop trust in your abilities to conquer the mountain. Michael Jordan, one of the world's greatest champions, missed more than 9,000 shots in his basketball career. He missed the game-winning shot 26 times. He also won six NBA championships because he believed he had the ability to make every shot he attempted. Despite missing the game-winning shot 26 times, his coaches and teammates believed he had the ability to make that shot every time. Michael Jordan was great at the small things. He mastered the mundane daily steps of his trade. As a result, he gave himself the opportunity to win championships. He conquered the mountain six times. When you trust in your ability to master the small steps of your life, you provide yourself with future opportunities to accomplish great achievements.

> *"Mediocrity is walking a tightrope while holding onto a handrail. Excellence is when you no longer need the handrail. Grandiosity is when you become the handrail. You become the handrail when you trust in your own abilities in such a manner that others lean on you to balance themselves as they walk the tightrope."*
>
> —Ronald T. Hickey

Some years ago, I owned a condominium unit in a large commercial complex. My unit was on the 11th floor. One evening, a female friend and I had returned from dining out to find the electrical power to the entire complex had been lost. The entire facility was pitch dark. I told my friend we would have to walk the entire 11 flights to get to my unit. She did not think that was such a good idea because she understood we would not be able to see where we were going. I told her not to be concerned because I could safely and securely find our way. She trusted me and took my hand. We entered the building from a street-level entry door and maneuvered our way to the 11th floor and directly to the door that accessed my unit. Once inside, I lit candles, and we reoriented our faculties. My friend expressed how impressed she was that I was able to find my way in complete darkness without making any wrong turns or causing injury to her or myself. I told her that while I served on board the USS Enterprise, we had to learn how to travel safely

PRINCIPLE NINE: EXPECTATIONS

to and from various locations within the ship in similar conditions. In the Navy, I was required, via scheduled emergency drill exercises, to practice and demonstrate my ability to move through the large aircraft carrier safely and securely. On a U.S. Navy ship, there are a variety of situations that would warrant everyone on board having the ability to travel about the ship in complete darkness. Your life could depend on your ability to get topside from 10 levels below deck in various locations during such emergencies as a fire. I felt this was such good training that it could save my life or someone else's life one day, even as a civilian. So, everywhere I lived, I trained myself to be able to travel in complete darkness throughout the building in case of any sort of emergency that required evacuation. The condominium complex was no exception. I had practiced on many occasions. So, when the night came to utilize my training, I was confident in my ability to safely and securely find my way to my unit in total darkness. To this day, I continue to practice this technique. The leadership lesson is this: Leadership in the workplace is often uncertain. Things happen that are simply beyond your control. During such times of uncertainty and challenge, you may sense you are blindly navigating with an urgency to survive safely and securely. You may be experiencing problems with personnel or processes. You may be in a situation where you are suddenly asked to assume a role of greater responsibility at work. You may have just gotten a new supervisor who is not sensitive to your needs as a professional. How well you have trained and prepared yourself to deal with life anomalies will ultimately establish the degree to which you trust your own abilities to see yourself through. If you trust your training and preparation, you will expect to handle all urgent matters with confidence and assuredness. I knew

I would safely get to my apartment in the dark. I was prepared; therefore, I expected to succeed. The degree to which you trust in your training, preparedness, and abilities will determine the efficacy of your efforts to move from point A to B with no detriment to your overall well-being. Leadership, oftentimes, requires executing in an environment of uncertainty, but the exceptional leader expects to succeed in the dark. Essentially, your abilities and the degree to which you trust your abilities are what determines the outcomes you will experience in every situation in life. You cannot always control the stimuli, but you control the response, unequivocally. The outcome is normally what you expect, or at least what you should expect. *Greatness Is What Greatness Does. Expectations are derived from your belief that you have the abilities to succeed at something. The greater you think of your abilities, the higher your expectations will be. You succeed when you expect to do so. You expect to do so when you believe you have the ability.*

If you cannot trust your own abilities or the abilities of your teammates to critically think to bring resolve to fundamental problems in your process patterns, you will never expect to reach your intended common destination, and your team will never experience the success that can only come from interdependency on one another. You will not succeed until you expect to succeed. Whether you consider your team to be your family, a group of coworkers, or social acquaintances you are engaged in a project with, your success depends on the self-sufficiency that only results from complete trust in one another's abilities. There are only a few things that are more counterproductive to success within a teamwork atmosphere than a person who does not trust their own abilities or the abilities of teammates.

PRINCIPLE NINE: EXPECTATIONS

Principle Nine Exercise: List the danger(s) in making the following statement:

"We do not know how to educate students of color in this current education system, which is built upon the tenets of White privilege and philosophies of White supremacy."

Build Expectation by Building Confidence in Your Abilities: List three things you can do to enhance your abilities to do the following:

- Create opportunities for increasing your leadership skills
- Bring resolve to fundamental problems you face at work
- Create trust between you and others in the workplace
- Overcome any obstacle that exists in your career pathway
- Remain progressive during times of extreme challenges
- Develop self-sufficiency without promoting isolation
- Succeed in your current workplace challenges

Principle Nine Challenge:
Blindfold yourself while seated at your desk in your office. Have someone ensure you remain safe from hazards or injuries. While completely blindfolded, walk safely to your vehicle. Repeat this challenge until you can trust your abilities to complete the challenge. Learn to expect success.
List five things you learned in the above challenge that you can implement at work to increase your leadership strengths.
List five things you learned in the above challenge that you can implement at work to weaken your leadership weaknesses.

PRINCIPLE TEN

Strategy

Strategy: The exceptional leader must have a strategic plan that guides and informs organizational behaviors. A properly designed strategy leads the organization along a value continuum that leads to a specific vision of success

> *"High-performing people in the workplace do not just happen. It takes a great people strategy to create them!"*
> —Ronald T. Hickey

Performance defines culture, and culture influences how leaders make people feel about their contributions to the workplace, the team, and the organization. It's about performance—not simply effort, but effectiveness. Great leaders don't measure staff by their effort but by what they produce in the organization's vital business. The exceptional leader measures staff by how much they produce, how effectively they produce it, and how efficiently they get their job responsibilities done. The best leaders strive to create a standard of excellence so that staff sense they are highly valued, and a great people strategy is the tool that creates such a workplace. I created a people strategy titled *ILLIMUNATE GREATNESS* to assist organizations in developing high-performing people and workforce standards of excellence. *ILLUMINATE GREATNESS* defines an organization's ambitious agenda for its workforce—*highly talented,*

PRINCIPLE TEN: STRATEGY

high-performing people with superb industry skills who strive for greatness and focus on excellence. This is the vision that *LLUMINATE GREATNESS* intends to achieve. Every strategy must have a vision it intends to achieve. *ILLUMINATE GREATNESS* aligns the eight ambitions of illumination with an organization's mission and bold strategic goals, drawing on the organization's responsibility to produce quality outcomes for the good of society.

The eight ambitions of illumination are as follows:

- *A – ATTRACT: Attract, hire, and retain the best people.*
- *M – MODEL: Model excellence – The world is watching.*
- *B – BEHAVIOR: Ensure excellent leadership behaviors.*
- *I – INSPIRE: Good enough is the enemy of best. Inspire greatness.*
- *T – TENACITY: Boldly create standards of excellence in everything you do.*
- *I – INCLUSION: Diversity, equity, and inclusion must be sustainable.*
- *O – OPEN: Open dialogue and open communication are the norm.*
- *N – NOW: "Right now" is our level of urgency in creating high expectations.*

By establishing these eight ambitions as a strategic focus in creating *"highly talented, high-performing people with superb industry skills who strive for greatness and focus on excellence,"* an organization defines its culture. And as stated above, culture influences how leaders make people feel about their contributions. Once you have defined your organization's ambitions, you must create the specific strategy steps that will guide and inform you in achieving the ambitions. I will use the first ambition, "ATTRACT," to provide an example of specific strategy steps I have helped organizations create.

The Ambition: Attract, Hire, and Retain the Best People

It's important that your organization can recruit from an energized and superbly skilled talent pool to attract the best people to assist your organization in achieving its business goals and objectives. Valuing high performance and excellence in the workforce can substantially impact your ability to be creative, innovative, and mission-driven and attract a workforce that will help you far exceed the needs and expectations of your organization. Your organization must be extremely attractive to the best talent available, and you must have a well-designed strategy for attracting, hiring, and retaining top talent. Your organization will struggle with all other goals of your operation if you struggle with this first ambition. Top talent is an absolute must for any organization striving for greatness.

Specific Steps:
1. *Use your strong brand to create an inspiring and motivating brand, harnessing the latest and best recruitment techniques, social media platforms, strategy partnerships, and other market-driven values to attract new top talent to enhance your organization and provide excellence in job performance.*
    a. *Brand your organization as a great workplace with great people.*
    b. *Offer and advertise your top compensation, rewards, and recognition.*

PRINCIPLE TEN: STRATEGY

    c. *Attract, hire, and retain only the best talent.*
    d. *Evaluate all employees annually, and do not retain poor performers.*
    e. *Incentivize current employees to recommend new top candidates.*
2. *Ensure you retain the right people in the right place at the right time, demonstrating the necessary skills and performance to meet your goals and objectives.*
    a. *Do whatever it takes to retain top talent.*
    b. *Provide growth opportunities within the organization for top talent.*
    c. *Understand what employees value the most and provide it.*

The above two steps, with sub-steps, are a template I have previously used and appear simple and basic, but very few organizations have a well-designed talent management strategy for attracting, hiring, and retaining top talent. Simply having a talent management team does not necessarily produce top talent for your organization. While some companies do well at attracting and hiring, it is rare to find a company that deploys a competitive strategy for retaining top performers. The goal of your talent management strategy should be to have a star player at every position in your organization. Like a professional sports team, you must recruit, select, develop, promote, and cut smartly, so you have only stars at every position. Your strategy must help you build a team of superstars committed to excellence. Cutting smartly is as critical as recruiting smartly if you are committed to having only superstars.

Now, you are ready to create your strategy for achieving the other seven ambitions in a similar fashion. Typically, this will involve bringing a smart collection of stakeholders together with a consultant to develop your overall people strategy. Along with the strategy, I suggest you offer your organization a clear set of behaviors and skills that you value as a leader. Establishing valued behaviors and skills is your way of communicating expectations to your team. The following are a set of seven valued behaviors and skills that I created for a public school district to offer district employees:

- *Passion for Students and Excellence in Education*
  - *You are deeply impassioned to the standards of excellence in public education values, and you inspire others around you to strive for and hunger for excellence in education as well.*
  - *You are extremely compassionate about the work we do at the district for our students, and your level of student value is infectious, addictive, and drives success.*
  - *You acknowledge the great accomplishments of your colleagues and the overall organization. You are quick to celebrate the success of others and look for win-win situations for the district and our students.*
  - *You have high expectations for success and lead your team with intellect, bravery, and tenacity, as you illuminate greatness in yourself and others, so the district exceeds our student's expectations.*
- *High Performance & Quality Academic Outcomes*
  - *You accomplish an enormous volume of quality and efficient work, and you demonstrate the ability to maintain a level of excellence in your job performance.*
  - *Your colleagues can rely on you because you consistently have high quality standards of job performance and drive yourself to be greater each day.*

PRINCIPLE TEN: STRATEGY

- *You focus solely on achieving quality results and meeting your own high expectations. You are mission-driven, not process-driven, achieving the best educational outcomes possible for our students.*
- *You take responsibility for your every action to ensure you remain on task and on schedule. You do not over analyze; you are highly productive and highly motivated. You NEVER shortcut quality.*

- *Illuminate Extraordinary Possibilities in Achievement*
  - *You thirst for knowledge and learn extremely quickly. Your capacity to ask questions is equal to your drive to improve your effectiveness in getting the job done and your curiosity for what is beyond the limits.*
  - *You are creative in your approach to learning and understanding how better to engage the district's strategic plan, students, policies, and procedures. You push yourself toward extraordinary possibilities.*
  - *You are increasingly curious about the business of education and how technology can be best applied to our people and education delivery processes. You creatively see beyond our standard processes and procedures. You envision extraordinary possibilities and strive for excellence in everything you do.*
  - *You do not limit yourself to your area of expertise. You constantly seek creative ways to contribute to the business of public education and think critically about the work others around you are doing.*

- *Tenacious Problem-Solving and Creative Thinking*
  - *You are constantly redesigning, reimaging, and reconfiguring processes, issues, and procedures to discover and rediscover improved or practical solutions to challenging problems and inefficient policies.*

- *You challenge "This is how we have always done it" and evaluate historical assumptions when you believe things can be done better and more effectively.*
- *You utilize your creative thinking and thought leadership to create new ideas and better process designs that generate useful nuances and solve challenging problems.*
- *You keep yourself and the organization agile and quick by eliminating unnecessary or complex problems. You work to simplify, clarify, improve, and solve problems.*
- Impeccable Integrity and Transparency
  - *You work with impeccable integrity and transparency and offer your great ideas because you know both are the exact cornerstones of excellence and high performance.*
  - *You take charge of challenging situations and make decisions that are not popular with integrity, transparency, and well-thought-out plans.*
  - *You challenge opinions, actions, and policies that are not consistent with our organizational culture of excellence, values of integrity, or objective goals.*
  - *You are willing to stand alone when you believe strongly that your views and/or smart risks are in the best interest of the district because you know you act with impeccable integrity.*
- Great Judgment in Diversity and Inclusion
  - *You make sound and wise decisions concerning people, processes, creativity, and business that have the greatest impact on the diversity and inclusion of students and staff.*
  - *You think strategically with diversity and inclusion in mind and can articulate why, how, and what you intend to accomplish, staying focused on the values of the district.*
  - *You discern wisely concerning diversity and inclusion and compartmentalize exactly what must be done now to move*

PRINCIPLE TEN: STRATEGY

the district smartly forward and make note of what can be improved upon to maximize organizational objectives and values.
- *You recognize diversity and inclusion problems before they occur and identify the root causes and develop a work resolution that gets the district beyond simply treating symptoms.*

- *Excellent Communication in Thought Leadership*
  - *You listen completely, and you are slow to react, so you are sure you have the best information that allows you to best understand. Your communications and actions are a mastery of thought leadership.*
  - *You are articulate and to the point in both verbal and written communication. You do not under or overcommunicate. Your communications are professional, clear, and concise and focused on the outcome.*
  - *You treat everyone with dignity and respect. Your level of communication conveys that you care about the well-being of others and the success of all district students and staff.*
  - *You are always in control of your emotions, so your communications are always appropriate, you speak with poise, and your verbal and written communications are void of any stress.*

With or without a strategy or clear set of valued behaviors and skills, organizations move ever forward on the timeline of the calendar, but they are constantly looking backward, seeking value and meaning, as deftly as any arrow seeking its target. Key performance indicators examine past employee productivity, seeking validation and assuredness that the organization will hit its target goals with the precision of an arrow hitting the bullseye. Back in classical Greece, the world's best philosophers figured out that the world is round and that atoms exist and philosophized that we can never prove what we know. One of these great thinkers from this era took up the notion of the "Paradox of the Arrow." His name was Zeno of Elea, and what he set forth can help us understand how relativity and quantum motions drive organizational success in a continuum. Zeno asked us to consider an arrow in flight, which he said, actually, cannot fly because at any one time, the arrow is at rest. In the arrow paradox, Zeno stated that for motion to occur, an object must change the position which it occupies. He used an arrow in flight to explain his theory. He stated that at any one instant of time, the arrow is neither moving to where it is at that very point nor moving to any point where it is not. However, it also travels within a distance in time to its destination, which means it is also, at any one time, in motion, or so it would appear to the human senses. The notion of the "Paradox of the Arrow" generates the question of whether the flight of an arrow in time is a unit or a continuum. Does it proceed in a granular (quantum) manner or as a steady uninterrupted stream? If granular, how are the points in time connected to create the illusion of constant motion? If the arrow moves as a continuous stream, how is the stream interrupted at any point in time? What's the relationship between organizational performance and the "Paradox of the Arrow?" The concept of strategy as a value continuum can be considered in a similar fashion. Does employee performance proceed in a granular (quantum) way or as a steady uninterrupted stream? If granular, how are the points of performance in time connected to create the illusion of constant motion (productivity)? If the employee performance moves as a continuous stream, how is the performance stream interrupted (production stops) at any point in time? Does absenteeism stop

PRINCIPLE TEN: STRATEGY

performance? Does attendance produce performance? What causes the arrow to travel a distance in time? What causes excellence in employee productivity in a unit of time? How are the points of performance in time connected to create the illusion that productivity is occurring?

Sufis are a mystical offshoot of Islamic religion, presented with the "Parable of the Blind Sufis," who together met an elephant for the first time. Each one was given the opportunity to touch the elephant and thereby understand what he was touching. One touched the tail and described the elephant likened to a rope. Another touched a leg and suggested that the elephant was like a tree trunk. Another touched the side of the elephant and concluded the elephant was like a concrete wall. One Sufi touched the elephant's ear and posited that an elephant is likened to a large piece of carpet. One touched the elephant's tusk and guessed a sharp spear, while another inspected the trunk and guessed the elephant was likened to a large snake. All were right, and all were wrong.

We all are like Zeno of Elea and the blind Sufis. We can only describe what we have experienced with our senses. Additionally, we imagine what we observe and experience as a still photo, when, in fact, it is an image moving in time. Our personal vision is a perspective and a point in time in the universal flow in organizational and individual performance. Fortunately, mathematics and instruments allow us to compare different aspects of the visible universe, improving our perception about it all. If all blind Sufis had been allowed to compare their individual observations with each of the other observations, they may have understood in greater accuracy the essence of an elephant. Thus, the challenge with strategies as a value continuum in time is that employees have a very limited understanding of the elephant because employees have a limited knowledge of the complete anatomy of the elephant. Substitute your organization for the elephant. Consider the arrow as an individual employee's performance.

The "Parable of the Blind Sufis" can be a clear visual, while we struggle with the dual concepts of classical and quantum mechanics when considering the flight of an arrow. Is the arrow moving or not, or doing both simultaneously? Are employees performing or not, or doing both simultaneously? Can one reality be dual? We need a concept that bridges the two. The bridge is "elasticity in performance." A rubber band stretches before it snaps. A stick bends before it breaks. Performance is the stretching and bending that occurs before the snap or break. A properly designed and implemented organizational strategy increases the "elasticity in performance" without causing a break in the quality of the performance. You cannot strategize a group of employees around the function of the elephant's ear if the group of employees have never touched the elephant's ear.

The organization is exactly as we perceive it. It is also exactly as everyone else perceives it. Can all perceptions create one reality, or do the individual perceptions of the organization create multiple realities of the organization? The goal of the organizational strategy is to take the various perceptions and create one common vision for everyone to follow. Therefore, what drives a culture of excellence? Your thought leadership and the quality of your people strategy drives the culture. If your organization does not have a people strategy that does not both inform and guide the relationships between the employer and the employees and between the employees and the work, then you are missing a great opportunity, and what happened at the Chernobyl nuclear power plant may be waiting to happen to you and your organization. What else encourages excellence in everything you do? Inspiring a common destination works. Challenging "good enough" works. Empowering others to act appropriately works. Team-building exercises to assist everyone in gaining knowledge of how to work better as a teamwork. Giving leaders the power to replace "low knowledge" and "low-performing" employees with "high knowledge" and "high-performing" employees works. High expectations work. Giving employees the freedom to grow and develop self-actualization in a creative and innovative environment works. Compassionate involvement in the lives of your teammates works. Preparing your professional operations and career development programs for unforeseen adversity works. Consistency of effort works. Rewards and incentives work. Exposing yourself, and those in your associations, to industry best practices and high standards work. Caring about the well-being of your staff works. Leading the way works. And having a well-designed strategy to guide and inform everyone's behavior works. These are all strategies that you can implement today to drive excellence in performance.

Strategically leading others toward a vision that produces the success you seek is the ultimate goal of leadership. A well-designed organizational strategy is the tool required to lead others toward a vision you have for the organization. Without a strategy, leadership is confined in a loop of behaviors that are reactive or transactional and tactical at best. You and your organizational operations will be constantly subjected to a chaotic environment defined by how well your team can react to and transact in various situations and circumstances that are never strategically associated with a particular vision specifically imagined for the success you desire. Michael Jordan had a vision for winning NBA championships from the very moment he stepped onto the court for the Chicago Bulls. His strategy was built on a value continuum that he never wavered from. He missed winning shots to prepare himself to make winning shots. In leadership, as in winning NBA championships, you keep taking the shots until your vision is realized. If you are not willing to take the shot, then you can never win. This is precisely why our experiences are what elevates us above our psychological constraints of always being in a reactive mode that leads to transacting with employees and staff. The workplace was never designed to be transactional in nature. Transactional work environments lead to self-centeredness, insecurities, feeling unsafe and unappreciated, egocentricity, and low self-esteem, eventually leading to employment dissatisfaction. This is also why no one knows the entire elephant. We work in noncollaborative silos, and we do not know whether the arrow is moving or standing still.

When the Chicago Bulls drafted Michal Jordan, the team had to have a strategy for making Michael satisfied as a member of the team. Because Michael Jordan was an extremely satisfied member of the Chicago Bulls, he played 13 of his 15 years in the NBA with the Chicago Bulls. When you, as a leader, hire a superbly talented star employee, what is your strategy for making that employee as satisfied as the Chicago Bulls made Michael Jordan? If we can design "people strategies" that guide and inform us on exactly how to make employees so satisfied that they spend their entire career in our organization, those people strategies will help us realize the vision of winning championships. This very notion demonstrates precisely the power and importance of having well-designed strategies that guide and inform our operations. If you have a vision for winning

PRINCIPLE TEN: STRATEGY

championships, I suggest you first study and learn what the Chicago Bulls did to make Michael Jordan satisfied and develop a comparable people strategy for your people.

Michael Jordan said: *"I've missed more than 9,000 shots in my career. I've lost almost 300 games. 26 times, I've been trusted to take the game-winning shot and missed. I've failed over and over and over again in my life. And that is why I succeed."*

Missing over 9,000 shots in his career was not Michael Jordan's strategy. Taking 20,000 shots was the strategy. Actions lead to experience, and experience allows learning from both successes and failures and pushes us forward. I don't know exactly where I stand on the dual reality of the arrow. Perhaps you don't either, but I do know that it's the upward climb toward personal self-satisfaction, based on our individual perspectives and perceptions, that determines what we become and just how we engage our vision along the way. Contemplating the "Paradox of the Arrow" is the beginning of the upward climb. No matter the outcome of endeavors, life will always provide a learning opportunity. It's up to us to squeeze every opportunity for all that the opportunity is worth. The exceptional leader understands this and learns to value failure as much as success as long as forward movement is gained along the value continuum. The value continuum is along the line of reaction, transaction, tactic, strategy, and vision. Having a strategy interrupts the repetitive reaction-transaction-tactic loop and pushes us toward our ultimate vision as units in time. Are you getting better as an organization over time? As Michael Jordan expressed in his quote, failure is as critical to success as triumph is, and missing a shot is not detrimental to your vision. In fact, missing from time to time becomes the very reason success is even possible because missing offers the opportunity to become better, and becoming better is the very purpose of having a strategy. Mastering the art of learning from experience requires leaders to constantly ask, "How can we do what we are doing in a more efficient and effective manner?" and "What can I do to make things better for my team?" Such questions create "elasticity in performance." The answers to these two critical questions provide the focus of your strategy. This continual examination process where you execute and then evaluate your results is the delineation that depicts your areas of success and your areas of opportunities. The idea is for leaders to move away from seeing anything as a mistake but rather an experience that provides an opportunity to learn and grow from along a value continuum. The continuum is not about what you are looking at but what you actually see as opportunity. As you learn from each experience, the contours of success should increase steadily over time because a great strategy also provides for a feedback loop that strengthens the overall strategy going forward. If your failure profile is consistently larger than your success profile, you are not learning from your mistakes, and you will find yourself in the perpetual motion of repeating mishaps, reacting and transacting continuously. Your strategy is not working at this point. If your operational strategies are designed well enough, mishaps will decline, and success will form the outlines of the vision of winning. Your strategy is pushing your vision into your reality, and that's exceptional leadership. Learning from your experiences is paramount for developing trust in your abilities and the abilities of those in your associations. With every championship your favorite sports teams have ever won, those championships occurred only after many missed shots were taken, countless plays were blown, and unintended mistakes were made. Winning is not a proposition of playing and executing perfectly but the result of which team misses the least number of shots and makes the fewest number of mistakes. For example, if you develop a well-designed talent management strategy for recruiting, hiring, and retaining the best talent in your industry, then your operations should eventually experience less disciplinary actions that result in terminating employees because, as a result of your talent management strategy, you will hire less poorly performing employees who need to be terminated.

*A **Quantum Psychology Perspective:** Understanding organizational strategy in the perspective of quantum psychology focuses on the individual contributor and how each employee views themselves in the greater scheme of operations. Most employees seek self-actualization as a basic human need. In psychology, self-actualization is achieved when one reaches their full potential in life. Therefore, being truly self-actualized is considered the exception, rather than the rule, because most people are consumed in trying to more urgently meet basic human needs, unfocused on the top of the pyramid. A strategy that leads to self-actualized employees is a strategy that wins championships. Psychologist Abraham Maslow outlines what is known as a hierarchy of human needs, identifying all the various needs that motivate and influence human behavior. Many have been exposed to Maslow's theories on human behavior in some capacity. The hierarchy of human need is often demonstrated by a pyramidal image, with the lowest levels of the pyramid representing basic human needs and more complex needs located at the top of the pyramid. The notion is that human behavior progresses up the pyramidal chart as people reach the different levels of basic security, safety, love, and esteem. At the peak of Maslow's hierarchy is self-actualization. The hierarchy suggests that when the other lower needs at the base of the pyramid have been met, one can focus their* *attention on this pinnacle human need of self-actualization. For instance, the basic need for food and shelter must be met before one can focus on other human needs. Once safety and security are met, one then can focus on egocentric, love, and self-esteem needs, such as rewards and recognition at work. Once human achievement has been fully realized, one then reaches the peak of self-actualization. There are several human characteristics of self-actualization:*

1. **Self-actualized people have emotional and psychological peak experiences.** One characterization of self-actualization is having frequent peak experiences. According to Maslow, a peak experience involves *"Feelings of limitless horizons opening up to the vision, the feeling of being simultaneously more powerful and also more helpless than one ever was before, the feeling of ecstasy and wonder and awe, the loss of placement in time and space with, finally, the conviction that something extremely important and valuable had happened, so that the subject was to some extent transformed and strengthened even in his daily life by such experiences."*

    In other words, these are peak emotional and psychological experiences in which a person feels their absolute best. A person, in some manner, is changed emotionally and transformed psychologically. Therefore, self-actualization can be looked upon as the vision one imagines when they describe the level of success one desires. As vision transcends the repeat loop of operating in a reactive, transactional, or tactical manner, self-actualization transcends the human behaviors created by food and shelter insecurities. In leadership, the leader must fully understand where within Maslow's human behavior pyramid he or she operates and where others under his or her leadership operate.

PRINCIPLE TEN: STRATEGY

This knowledge is critical to designing operational strategies. Who we are matters.

2. **Self-actualized people accept who they are and possess an inclusive global view of the world.** Self-actualized people accept their mistakes and wrongdoings and accept others as they are. They tend to be free-spirited and intuitive and can enjoy their lives without guilt or regret. Self-actualized people treat all people the same regardless of background, financial or social status, or other socioeconomic and cultural factors.

3. **Self-actualized people focus only on realism.** Being realistic is another characteristic of self-actualized people. Rather than being fearful of failure, mistakes, or the unknown, self-actualized people view life as it truly is in its logical and rational forms.

4. **Self-actualized people are problem-solvers.** This is one major characteristic that causes self-actualized people to be great leaders. Self-actualized individuals are often guided by a strong sense of personal ethics and moral responsibility. They enjoy problem-solving and helping other people improve their own lives. They are other people centered.

5. **Self-actualized people are very independent and tend to live a solitary life.** Self-actualized people also tend to be isolated. They seldom conform to other people's ideas of them. Their independent perspective allows them to live in the moment and appreciate the opportunity each experience presents.

"Few people even scratch the surface, much less exhaust the contemplations of their own experiences."
—Randolph Bourne

Creating a well-designed people strategy for your organization will allow your organization to embrace new ways of operating, focusing on the benefits of attracting top talent and using the latest technology to drive productivity and performance. The people strategy will work in partnership with the strategic plan to ensure the organization has a highly skilled and high performance-focused workforce. The newly created working environment will be inclusive, collaborative, forward-thinking, agile, and efficient, fostering innovation, creativity, and standards of excellence in performance. Senior leaders will possess strong inspirational leadership. Engaged employees will understand your vision and the impact their valuable performances produce. All employees will illuminate greatness. Employees will be self-actualized and empowered to act and think, working skillfully and collaboratively across the organization, and embrace and celebrate excellence in performance in everything they do. Greatness Is What Greatness Does.

www.ingramcontent.com/pod-product-compliance
Lightning Source LLC
Chambersburg PA
CBHW061545140625

28087CB00007B/15